HOW TO
GRADUATE
DEBT
FREE

Published by Worthy Publishing, a division of Worthy Media, Inc., One Franklin Park, 6100 Tower Circle, Suite 210, Franklin, Tennessee 37067.

HELPING PEOPLE EXPERIENCE THE HEART OF GOD
eBook available at www.worthypublishing.com

Library of Congress Cataloging-in-Publication Data

Names: Ellis, Kristina, author.
Title: How to graduate debt free : the best strategies to pay for college / Kristina Ellis.
Description: Franklin, Tennessee : Worthy Publishing, 2016.
Identifiers: LCCN 2016018057 | ISBN 9781617957437 (paperback)
Subjects: LCSH: College costs—United States. | Education—United States—Finance. | Scholarships—United States. | Student aid—United States. | Finance, Personal—United States. | BISAC: STUDY AIDS / Financial Aid.
Classification: LCC LB2342 .E436 2016 | DDC 378.3/8—dc23
LC record available at https://lccn.loc.gov/2016018057

Scripture quotation taken from *The Message.* Copyright © 1993, 1994, 1995, 1996, 2000, 2001, 2002. Used by permission of NavPress Publishing Group.

The personal stories in this book are all used by permission. Terry Looper's testimonial in chapter 1 derives from an unpublished manuscript. Portions of chapter 5 are drawn from Kristina Ellis's first book, *Confessions of a Scholarship Winner,* published by Worthy Publishing, copyright © 2013. Used by permission. To the best of the author's knowledge, the statistics and advice in this book were accurate at the time of publication.

For foreign and subsidiary rights, contact rights@worthypublishing.com

ISBN: 978-1-61795-743-7 (trade paper)

Cover Design: Chris Tobias
Author photos © Marisa Mlynarek

Printed in the United States of America
16 17 18 19 20 LBM 8 7 6 5 4 3 2 1

Praise for *How to Graduate Debt-Free*

"Kristina shoots straight about what you need to do to maximize the opportunities to pay for college. This book is a surefire resource for anyone who dreams of a debt-free degree. Every high school and college student should have a copy."

Farnoosh Torabi

Personal Finance Author; Host of the Award-winning Podcast So Money

"In her book, Kristina gives practical, actionable, and effective advice for students looking to attend and pay for college. A great read for all students, especially low-income and first-generation students who may not have access to this information otherwise. Her personal story is also very inspiring."

Christopher Gray

Co-founder & CEO at Scholly; Forbes 30 under 30 Honoree

"Kristina's real-life experience in navigating the scholarship process and the practical knowledge she gives to families and students will guide them toward a debt-free college education. The information in this book just works. I knew there should be an easy way to explain the approaches to paying for college without accumulating debt, and this is it."

Traci O. Aucoin

GEAR UP Project Director

"Kristina Ellis has done it again with her latest book, *How to Graduate Debt-Free*. This is a powerful book, covering all the topics that parents and future college students must understand in order to minimize college debt. This is a timely book that will open up your eyes."

Tom Corley

CPA; Best-selling Author of
Rich Habits, Rich Kids and Change Your Habits, Change Your Life

"I've been helping high school students get into college for over 20 years, and I learned about several new resources from *How to Graduate Debt-Free*. This is not simply a book but a conversation starter. Buy several copies and you will get parents and students alike talking about innovative ways to reduce their college expenses."

Andrew Morrison

COO of Mentoring in Medicine

"This book is both a springboard and a compass. It will help students and families dive into the often-confusing realm of college funding and point to the true north of how to plot the journey. A must-read for the college-bound."

Sheila Graber

School Counselor

"I can confidently say, this book really drives home the importance of graduating college debt-free. Kristina's easy-to-read book is packed full of resources, guidelines, financial principles, and how-to's, yet it is laid out in a way that makes total sense! Anybody who's ever felt they need help paying for college or learning how it all works will really benefit from this real-world information."

Chance

College Sophomore

HOW TO
GRADUATE
DEBT
FREE

KRISTINA ELLIS

WORTHY®
PUBLISHING

CONTENTS

A NOTE TO READERS

To be honest . . . when I first began my paying-for-college journey, I had no clue what strategies were available. It was such an overwhelming feeling to be staring at a mountain of college costs and have no idea where to start. Naturally, I assumed that if my family didn't have enough money upfront, my dreams just might not happen.

Little did I know how wrong my assumptions were! There are so many different ways to pay for college. If you're willing to put in the time, effort, and forethought, you can make it happen.

To me, this quest is like an entrepreneur who's seeking funding for a new business. While some entrepreneurs find the money right away, many more have to remain relentlessly determined to try multiple approaches to secure what their company needs to get to that next level. In either case, the benefits of that investment pursuit can be massive!

Don't be intimidated if you are at the bottom of your

own mountain and have no idea how you're going to scale it. Together in the coming pages, we will explore numerous tips, strategies, and techniques to help you develop a personalized plan for conquering obstacles and reaching the top. My hope for you is that you not only get the degree and the career you dream of, but that you accomplish it in a way that sets you up for financial freedom and success throughout your lifetime.

I believe in you more than you know, and I'm excited to be on this journey with you.

Let's get started!

Kristina Ellis

#NOTGOINGBROKE

There I stood, trying to catch my breath. Waves of fear and intimidation swept through me as my mom finished her sentence: "You have four years to figure out what you're going to do with your life, because you're on your own financially after you graduate high school."

I don't know why she's telling me this, I thought. *I'm just a freshman! What can I do about it?* But before I had the chance to snap back, she went on to explain, "Kristina, I'm telling you this because I love you, and I believe in you. And I know that if you work hard now, you can go to a great college."

The truth was, as a single mother of two, she didn't have the money to pay for my education. She was running a hair salon out of our home and doing the best she could to get by, but she knew it wouldn't be enough. So even though her words were hard to choke down in that moment, I knew she was just trying to help. In fact, by telling me that day, she did me an enormous favor: giving me the time to devise a strategy and start planning. Ultimately, I was able to win over $500,000 in scholarships and graduate from my dream school, Vanderbilt University, as well as continue on to earn a master's degree—completely debt-free.

Beyond Scholarships

I shared the rest of my story—and my secrets to scholarship success—in my first book, *Confessions of a Scholarship Winner*, because I wanted to give every student not only a vision for the future but a strategy to make their college dreams come true. Since then, I've had the opportunity to travel the country teaching thousands of students and parents how to achieve their own scholarship success. Yet even with the most engaged audiences, I still get asked, "But Kristina . . . if I *don't* win scholarships, can I still pay for college?"

I wish I could answer, "Don't worry; everyone can get a full ride!" However, the reality is that only a small percentage of students will receive enough scholarship money to cover the entire cost of college. So where does that leave everybody else who dreams of a degree? For those families who can't realistically cover it all out of pocket, and for students who don't want to spend years tied down by massive debt, is it still possible to graduate debt-free? The answer is YES! There are plenty of ways.

I've written *this* book to lay out the numerous approaches

to paying for college and to show you that no matter your situation, if you're motivated, you can get that degree without going into debt!

While this dream may seem like an impossible feat, I'm here to say it is not only possible—but well within your reach! Sure, there's a lot to think through and follow up on: evaluating the best ways to save for school, taking the tests that need to be completed before you ever step foot on campus, filling out financial aid applications, and various other details. But it's totally doable!

Take a deep breath and realize: it's not the end of the world if you don't get everything perfect. There's a lot to do, but we can work through it together—one step at a time. With determination, the right information, and a well-planned strategy, you can earn that career-advancing degree and graduate from college **#NotGoingBroke**!

Invest in Yourself

Before we get started, I want to issue you a challenge: commit to investing in yourself. Most great opportunities require some sort of investment, and there is no greater opportunity than your future.

People typically view investments strictly from a financial sense, but time is money, too, and the hours you spend laying the groundwork now can lead to thousands of dollars in savings and a much higher earning potential in the future.

Whether you're a senior in high school, a parent with a child in elementary school, or a professional returning for an advanced degree, taking the time to learn some foundational financial principles and become savvy about the various aspects of college finance will increase your chances of graduating from your dream school debt-free.

So make a commitment that, regardless of your financial status or the obstacles that may stand in your way, you *will* invest the necessary time and energy in yourself and your future. I promise . . . YOU ARE WORTH IT!

Now let's get started and get you on your way to graduating debt-free!

1

A WINNING MONEY MINDSET

Setting the Foundation

The best investment you can make is in yourself.

Warren Buffett

I took one look and I knew I was in love. I dreamed of all the memories we would make and the fun we would have together ...

The first time I saw that trampoline commercial, there was no doubt: it had to be mine. My big brother felt the same way—we just *had* to have one. The problem was, at three and five years old, we didn't have any money.

When Mark and I approached our parents, Mom and Dad quickly informed us they had no plans to purchase a trampoline. Instead we were told: "When you can think of how to make the $200 to buy one, you can get it."

Upon hearing this, my brother, who is now a biomedical

and cloud-computing engineer, immediately pulled me into his room and said, "Kristina, we have to make a plan."

As he and I brainstormed, we put together our strategy: we would sell homemade cookies and lemonade during the upcoming Rendezvous, our town's biggest event, held annually over Memorial Day weekend. We told our parents, and they got on board. Our mom agreed to help us make our "product," and we rehearsed the best sales pitches we could come up with.

During that weekend, we sat in the front yard behind our makeshift sales counter for more than 20 hours over two days. Even though it was hot outside and our friends were off enjoying the festivities, we refused to leave our post as long as there were potential customers nearby. On Sunday evening, when the sun went down and Dad pulled out the moneybox, we sat at the kitchen table, gripping the wooden edges and nervously awaiting our total. We hadn't reached our $200 goal by day's end on Saturday, so we felt especially anxious for the final results.

When he finished counting, Dad took a deep breath and said, "So that's it."

I thought, *So that's* what?

"You made $327!" he announced.

"We did it!" Mark and I screamed.

Amid our high fives and happy dances, something else suddenly occurred to us: not only could we get a trampoline, but we could buy something else *major* with our extra $127! We ended up purchasing both our trampoline *and* a basketball goal—well beyond what we had imagined—for one weekend of combined work!

In that moment, far more than the dream of a trampoline was realized. Deep within me, a money mindset—and a lifelong conviction—was formed: with hard work and a winning strategy, any financial obstacle can be overcome.

10 Can't-Miss Financial Principles

Over the years I've learned many additional lessons in financial strategy—some of them through research and study, and a lot of them in the laboratory of real life. Underlying them all is the need for a bedrock of financial understanding. Before I can help you determine how to pay for college, it's important that we lay a strong foundation that will stand the test of time. These principles will help you enact a great strategy to both graduate debt-free *and* achieve financial success throughout your lifetime.

....

PRINCIPLE #1:
START EARLY

....

Procrastination seems to be a part of human nature. Most people fight it at least some of the time, including me. As tempting as it can be to put off things until they're absolutely necessary, the sooner you begin working toward any goal, the greater your chances of success. Especially with finances.

Starting early can help you get ahead in many ways. Not only does it allow for money principles like compound interest to work hugely in your favor (see Principle #5 below), but it gives you more time to implement effective strategies, which will reduce stress. It also helps with things like applying for college and scholarships. Many students wait until senior year to think about applications, but most admission and scholarship award decisions are based on your entire high school experience, beginning with ninth grade. Students who begin planning early, even as early as junior high, have the advantage of extra time to go after big goals and develop a winning résumé.

Getting Ahead

Terry Looper, founder and CEO of Texon—a multibillion-dollar energy marketing company in Houston—prepared for a high level of success his entire life. The 2012 Ernst & Young Entrepreneur of the Year explains, "I was so enthusiastic about someday being in business that at age six, I aspired to own my own company, simply because I knew of a man in my little Texas town who owned a men's clothing store. Early on, I also realized the impact an impressive résumé could have, and so, beginning in middle school, I intentionally made choices that would position me to appeal to future employers."

First and foremost, Looper got involved in almost every service organization and school club possible, and he sought to be a leader in each of them. By the time he was in high school, he was president of his class, vice president of the student body, treasurer of the Key Club (a service organization), and a regular in his church youth group, among other activities. In college he went on to be vice president of his fraternity, as well as student president of the engineering department. He also worked two jobs for extra income, including running a coin-operated foosball table business.

A few years after graduation, when the opportunity came for him to help run a start-up, he was ready. And later, when it was time to found his own company, he went for it— knowing he'd *planned for it* his entire life. He is living proof that it can pay, in so many ways, to start early.

If you didn't get moving as early as you wish you had, don't be down on yourself, but also understand: waiting won't make it any better. I encourage you to fight any urge to keep putting things off and instead work on tackling your financial goals immediately. It's never too late to strategize and launch from where you are. With each new day you have the opportunity to positively impact your savings and earning potential, so start now.

PRINCIPLE #2:

MAKE A PLAN

Pioneer aviator Antoine de Saint-Exupéry once said, "A goal without a plan is just a wish." It's safe to say most people want to be financially secure throughout their lives. In fact, almost everyone dreams of having enough money to never have to worry about bills again. But as many prosperous people will tell you, wealth doesn't come easily. Yes, there are the few lottery winners and occasional celebrities who reach overnight fame, but they're the exceptions. Most often, the journey to financial success requires deliberate choices and long-term thought. So take an honest look at your finances and make a game plan.

You may be thinking, *I'm only a sophomore in high school . . . What do I have to worry about?* The reality is, you're in charge of your financial future, and your future starts now. While your parents may be helping you, the level of financial success you'll achieve is ultimately up to you. Plenty of college graduates have tumbled headfirst into a canyon of overwhelming student loan debt, never expecting that they would still be trying to climb out of it 10 or 20 years later.

At this moment, you have the opportunity to avoid such a pit. Think through which financial goals you *need* to reach in each of the next five years to achieve your college dreams (this book will help you figure those out)—and then which financial goals you *want* to accomplish even 10 years from now. Then sit down and write out what it will take to make them happen. Include things you can do on a month-to-month and year-to-year basis to keep you on track. And don't forget to implement daily habits to support your efforts. Perhaps this month you can apply for three scholarships, and today you can skip that $4 coffee at Starbucks so that *next year* you'll have not only some scholarship money reserved in your name but a certain amount of savings set aside.

Be sure to celebrate milestones along with small wins throughout the process to mark your progress and help you stay motivated. Creating your financial plan may take a little time upfront, but it can quite literally pay off in the long run.

PRINCIPLE #3:
CREATE AND MAINTAIN A BUDGET

Keep an eye on the money you have coming in and going out. Best-selling author John Maxwell says, "A budget is telling your money where to go instead of wondering where it went." As simple as this sounds, a recent Gallup poll revealed that only 30 percent of Americans track their income and expenditures. Not monitoring your spending habits can cause you to pay out significantly more than you anticipated, further distancing you from your goals. Especially since college often turns out to be far more costly than families expect.

A multitude of extra expenses can creep up before you know it. From test and application fees to deposits, campus visits, and dorm room supplies, there will be no shortage of opportunities to spend . . . and spend . . . and spend. So know what you can afford by creating and living on a budget. By facing your financial situation head-on, you'll be better able to anticipate and prepare for future expenses, as well as avoid impulse purchases.

See chapter 9 for more information on how to set up and maintain a budget.

PRINCIPLE #4:
AVOID DEBT

As you make contact with colleges and universities, you will be pitched some crazy tuition rates—the kinds of numbers that most families can't even begin to imagine coming up with on their own. These schools know, however, that the "debt industry" stands ready to provide the funds for parents and students to borrow their way through. However, beware the real price tag—this money is never cheap!

Debt is borrowed funds that have to be paid back, most often with interest. "With interest" means a percentage is added to your balance each month to compensate the lender for delaying repayment. Ultimately, you will end up paying back more—sometimes much more—than you initially borrowed. Financial guru and best-selling author Dave Ramsey describes it in these terms: "The decision to go into debt alters the course and condition of your life. You no longer own it. You are owned."

Sadly, the business of debt has left too many people trapped in a desperate cycle that is hard to escape. For example, if you borrow $100,000 in student loan debt at a 6.8 percent interest rate with a 10-year term, then you will not only be paying back the principal—the original money you borrowed—but also an extra $38,097 in interest over the duration of the loan!

$100,000 Loan @ 6.8% Interest for 10 years	
Total Interest Paid	$38,096.57
Total Amount Repaid	$138,096.57
Monthly Payment	$1,150.80

Paying back $1,150 per month, on top of other living expenses, isn't realistic or even remotely possible for most new graduates. Keep this in mind too: after graduation, you'll have even more opportunities to sink further into debt as you're offered store credit cards, car loans, introductory cash bonuses "just for signing up," and so on. Therefore, be very wary. While there are some rare times to take on what is deemed "good debt" (such as a mortgage to buy a home), debt most often causes far more harm than good and should be strongly avoided.

For more information on how to navigate debt, especially student loans, see chapter 7.

PRINCIPLE #5:
USE THE POWER OF COMPOUND INTEREST

You've probably heard people mention how "the rich keep getting richer." Well, compound interest is a powerful financial tool that has a lot to do with that notion. Depending on whether it's working for you (through savings or investments) or against you (in a loan), it can tremendously multiply wealth over time—or cause you to lose it faster than you thought possible.

When your money is already earning interest, and then that interest earns additional interest, you're seeing the positive side of compounding at work: it's *money making money*. In the case of a loan, this works against you when the interest on your debt keeps increasing your debt.

Albert Einstein has been credited with saying, "The power of compound interest is the most powerful force in the universe. He who understands it . . . earns it. He who doesn't . . . pays it." If you want to see the huge difference compound interest can make, search for an online "savings calculator" and see what $5,000 or $10,000 today will look like 40 years from now at a 6.5 percent interest rate. Now take that same figure and imagine you borrowed it at that interest rate. The several thousand dollars gained by saving could just as quickly be lost through borrowing.

Evaluate each dollar for what it can benefit or cost you in the long run. The earlier you grasp this concept and start using it to your advantage, the more time your money has to make money for you.

. . . .

PRINCIPLE #6:
PAY YOURSELF FIRST
. . . .

Renowned finance expert Robert Kiyosaki—often called "The Millionaire Schoolteacher"—advises, "You must have the self-discipline to pay yourself first." He goes on to explain the importance of setting aside income for savings and investments *before* your paycheck disappears to bills and extras you don't really need. This way, you have money to invest in assets that can earn more money for you!

Make a habit of immediately putting aside a certain amount of everything you make. For example, if you know you're going to get paid $100 for mowing lawns this weekend, you could determine in advance that you'll put $20 of it into an interest-earning account. This will help you avoid the temptation to spend it all when your friends start buying the latest video games or tech gadgets. Following this principle makes growing your savings a top priority and increases your potential for reaching financial freedom.

PRINCIPLE #7:

VALUE YOUR TIME

Time wasted comes at a cost. In fact, financially speaking, it's often described in terms of *opportunity cost*—which Investopedia.com defines as "the cost of an alternative that must be forgone in order to pursue a certain action." In other words, for every hour you spend on a particular activity, you're giving up the opportunity to spend that hour doing something else. You can gain or lose a lot simply by valuing or not valuing your time.

For example, if you could graduate from college in four years, but you take six years instead, you lose not only whatever it costs you to attend school for those two additional years (which could easily be well over $50,000 in tuition and fees), but you forfeit the income you could have made during that time. According to the National Association of Colleges and Employers, the average starting salary for a college graduate was $48,127 in 2014. Therefore, that additional two years in school could equate to about $100,000 in lost earnings—and another $50,000 or so that the extra schooling cost you!

Time is money, so be intentional with how you spend it. You'll not only increase your financial fitness, but you'll build your life around things that energize you and bring you happiness.

Work Smarter, Not Harder

Efficient work almost always beats strenuous work. A long-ago Chrysler executive once said, "I will always choose a lazy person to do a difficult job . . . because he will find an easy way to do it." Perhaps you're considering putting together an elaborate filing system with lots of paperwork and folders when an online app could do the same thing in a fraction of the time. Or you're thinking about touring 20 college campuses when a virtual tour would suffice for all but your top schools. Think through areas of your life where you can smartly increase efficiency so you can focus your efforts on the things that matter most and that move you even further forward.

PRINCIPLE #8:

DON'T OVERPAY

Why pay more when you can pay less? As simple and cliché as that may sound, it's a valid question. If you can find the same item or service for much cheaper, with only a little extra research and patience, why not spend less and save your cash?

For most college students, money is tight. Any chance to keep some of it in your pocket and make your dollars stretch is a win. With a multitude of websites and apps designed to help you locate the best price on just about anything, getting a deal is easier now than ever. Keep an eye out for discount codes, coupons, and sales. While 15 percent off or "buy one, get one" may seem inconsequential in the moment, it all adds up. Just remember to use deals on things you actually need; don't buy something simply because it's "on sale."

Over the years, practicing this principle has allowed me to enjoy a lifestyle far beyond my income. I've spent a month traveling through Europe at nearly 70 percent off standard retail price. I've furnished my home with new, high-end furniture I found at a 90 percent discount. And just last week I saved $100 repairing the brakes on my car simply by remembering to print off a coupon before I left the house. With just a little extra effort, I've saved thousands!

Also, always be willing to negotiate or bargain. In an interview with *Inc.* magazine, serial entrepreneur and venture capitalist Howard Tullman stated, "My rule of thumb is that someone is going to have the best seat in the house. It may not be me. But shame on me if I don't ask for it."

His words really changed my approach to negotiating. In many situations, it's completely acceptable to ask for a better price. Most people simply accept the number put in front of them to avoid feeling uncomfortable. I encourage you, though, to develop negotiation skills and be unafraid to give bargaining a shot. You may not end up with anything better ... or you just might get the deal of a lifetime. But you'll never know unless you ask!

Though it's not at all the norm, there have even been situations where students have gone so far as to negotiate with their college for a better financial aid package—and succeeded! I know of a high school senior who had been accepted to multiple schools and was offered $18,000 in grants and scholarships by his second choice but only $5,000 in free money by the one he really wanted to attend. The student spoke with a financial aid officer at his top pick, explaining his situation and requesting an offer that more closely matched the other one's package. As a result of that conversation, the dream school upped its offer by an additional $10,000 in gift aid! While this doesn't always happen, and shouldn't be expected, that student took a risk that really paid off!

....

PRINCIPLE #9:
CONSIDER ROI BEFORE YOU BUY

What is the value you'll get back from something you invest in, and is it worth the cost? For example, if you decide to spend your time hanging out with a particular friend, you probably expect some sort of positive return, like a fun evening or the happiness you feel when you're around that person. It's not likely you'd choose to spend hours upon hours with someone who makes you miserable. You'd be yielding a negative *return on investment* (ROI), meaning that what you got back from that hangout was not worth what you gave up for it.

The ROI is simply the benefit you receive from investing in someone or something. In the context of this book, you especially want to consider your financial ROI in advance of any major purchase, because every dollar you spend elsewhere is one less dollar toward being debt-free when you graduate. For example, before you buy that car for school or choose a meal plan, evaluate how much bang you'll get for your buck. Will the item you're considering bring enough additional value to your life to justify the cost? Or is there an alternative that makes more sense financially? This is especially important to consider when looking at which college you'll "purchase," because the stakes are high and long lasting.

In chapter 8, we'll discuss how to effectively evaluate a college's ROI for yourself.

PRINCIPLE #10:

LIVE GENEROUSLY

If you want to see good multiply, live generously. Giving back to make the world a better place with your time, your talent, and your treasure (money and material possessions) is important. Proverbs 11:24 in *The Message* Bible sums it up well: "The world of the generous gets larger and larger; the world of the stingy gets smaller and smaller."

A giving mindset can have such a powerful effect, not only making life better for others but also for you. According to the book *The Paradox of Generosity*, sociologists have found that generous people tend to be in better health and experience less depression. Therefore, when adopting and developing your own money principles, purposely think through how you want to give back. Those who live generously live well—and are truly rich.

Get Your Game On

When it comes to money, there's a lot to learn, and the growth curve never ends. You'll constantly be discovering what works for you and how you want your financial picture to look. The most important thing is to be intentional about your money: how you think about it, what you do with it, and what you make it do for you.

Building a strong foundation will not only help as you prepare to pay for college—one of the biggest expenditures in your young-adult life—but it will also set you up for success in all money-related areas once you're out of college and living in the real world. Since financial struggles are a leading cause of divorce and stress-related issues, getting your money game on now can empower you to live a much happier, healthier life. So put these principles to use and start establishing your own winning ways.

SUMMARY POINTS

▶ It's important to lay a strong foundation of financial understanding that will stand the test of time. This will not only help you enact a great strategy to pay for college but enable you to achieve financial success throughout your lifetime.

▶ The bedrock financial principles are: Start Early, Make a Plan, Create and Maintain a Budget, Avoid Debt, Use the Power of Compound Interest, Pay Yourself First, Value Your Time, Don't Overpay, Consider ROI Before You Buy, and Live Generously.

2

SAVING FOR COLLEGE

Preparing the Way

An investment in knowledge pays the best interest.

Benjamin Franklin

It's common knowledge that saving money throughout your lifetime is a great idea. I could spend several paragraphs spouting clichés about the wisdom of saving, but since you're reading this, I have a feeling you already know it's important. The real trick for most people is actually doing it.

Studies show that only about one-third of Americans have more than $1,000 in their savings accounts. But don't let that scare you. You are totally capable of doing what it takes—and in fact, you have the potential to be a great saver! So I challenge you, before we dive into the details, to first assume and expect that you are able to save. Even if you do so in very small increments to start with, your dimes will turn into dollars in no time.

If you're already in college or getting ready to go in the near future, and you don't have a big savings account, don't be discouraged by this chapter. While having the time and ability to save in advance is ideal, this is just one of many strategies in this book to help you graduate debt-free. Still, go ahead and read these pages. Learning to save as you move into the future has the power to change everything! It can give you freedom in your finances for the rest of your life. And that alone is worth investing toward.

Where Will the Money Come From?

How exactly do you go about finding the additional funds to put aside for college? If your parents are on a set salary and/or living paycheck to paycheck, the prospects of your family saving extra may seem slim. Well, take heart; there are many ways to build a college fund. With a little awareness and strategic planning, finding money for that purpose can quickly become a reality.

After you've finished this chapter, why not sit down with your parents and discuss the possibilities for you as a family? Brainstorm some ideas on your own beforehand, and then go over them during your conversation. Together, you could come up with all kinds of creative ways to ease a tight budget. And showing your parents that you're also willing to make sacrifices can go a long way as well.

When it comes to savings, advice from financial experts tends to fall into two broad categories: *cut back* or *earn more*. The first category takes more of a minimalistic, budget-focused approach; the second category encourages the pursuit of additional income that can be deposited into savings. There's not a right or wrong option. Many people have found a blend of the two to work best; it really just depends on your personal situation and schedule.

CUTTING BACK

The easiest way to put money aside in savings is to wisely spend what you already have coming in and cut back wherever you can. Within your overall budget, where can you as a family—and you personally—be a little more strategic to gain some ground?

- Perhaps you can skip out on a guilty pleasure like going to a movie every weekend and go once a month instead. Or get your movies through Redbox or Netflix.
- Maybe you could swap certain things for a cheaper version, such as exchanging your game-day pizza delivery for making one at home. Or three days a week, everyone could take their lunch to school or work rather than eating out.

- Can you use less electricity around the house by un-plugging appliances or turning down the thermostat?
- If you live in a city, how about opting for public transportation or riding a bike instead of taking on a car payment, insurance, and gas?

Think through what's most important, write out your priorities in order, and then evaluate which bottom-of-the-list items you can do without or get by with less of.

You're likely to pinpoint at least a few things to help you work toward your goal. Even saving $50 a month makes a difference over time, especially if you're taking advantage of compound interest. In fact, when you really start scrutinizing what you can reduce or eliminate, the amount that stays in your pocket may be pretty surprising.

This approach works well for many families, particularly when they don't have time to devote to the other approach: identifying additional income opportunities.

EARNING MORE

The second major line of thought—earning more—is also a great savings solution, though it can look very different depending on your situation. Perhaps you're a high school student who wants to take on a part-time or summer job. Or maybe you're a parent or adult student intending to ask for a raise or leverage your skills to pursue a higher-paying job. You may even be thinking about a side project or a new business altogether. Whatever your additional income source, be diligent to immediately set aside extra money toward savings. It can be tempting to spend more as you earn more, increasing your lifestyle or going on a shopping spree; however, pay yourself first by putting away the money in savings.

Sweet Jobs for High School Students

High school students take on jobs for a variety of reasons—most often to pay for everyday expenses. And while covering the necessities is great, a lot of high school students use their money for extras that aren't really that important. Think through your long-term goals and reserve some of that cash for college. From working at a local fast-food joint to mowing lawns to starting a babysitting business, a variety of jobs are available. But let me challenge you to go one better: rather than just finding any job, search for work in your field of interest, or a position that offers unique and interesting growth experiences. These types of opportunities provide a dual benefit: savings for college, and a more competitive college and scholarship résumé.

Most schools and scholarship programs evaluate your extracurricular activities when you apply; therefore, having a job that shows you're working toward your future goals and displaying an extra level of responsibility can help you stand out from the competition. For example:

- Maybe you're planning to study education and become a teacher. Then consider working at a youth summer camp or starting a babysitting business while in high school.

- Do you aspire to become a CEO or business leader? Think about how to set up your work like a business. If you're mowing lawns, then have a billing system, organize your finances, hire extra help during crunch times, and be creative in how you market yourself and acquire customers. Then, when you apply for college, you'll have this experience to feature on your résumé. My brother did just that. And when he left for school, he was able to sell his client book for lawn mowing to another aspiring entrepreneur in our area.

- I got a job at our local gymnastics facility and worked my way up to being head coach of the gymnastics team. Not only did that position allow me to earn money that could be saved for college, it also gave me leadership experience to include on my college and scholarship applications.

If you're highly involved in extracurricular activities throughout the school year but still want a job, take advantage of extra time during the summers. There is plenty of seasonal work available, like being a lifeguard, golf caddy, or camp counselor.

In case you can't find the perfect opportunity, remember: you can make any job a premium experience by going above and beyond what's asked of you. Don't do the minimum; work to be the very best at what you do. Even if you don't have a great title, exercising an extra level of commitment and initiative displays qualities that colleges love to see. At the same time, you'll be getting closer to your debt-free goals.

Beyond earning more through a job, what about trying some other ways to make cash for college? One idea is to sell the stuff you don't need. Maybe you have a baseball card collection, clothes, jewelry, or electronics you don't and won't use anymore. If you're moving into a dorm, you probably won't be able to take everything with you anyway, so let your stuff work for you now. Take inventory of what you're willing to get rid of and find a way to get money for it. Websites such as eBay, OfferUp, craigslist, and a multitude of apps make it easier than ever to earn extra cash for your extras.

Or consider having a good old-fashioned yard sale. Ask friends and family if they will donate items that you can sell, allowing you to keep the proceeds for school. You might even post word of the event online as well as in your community, letting people know this is a college fund-raiser. Customers will often pay more—or even throw in a little extra donation—in support of your goal because they know it's going toward a good cause.

Another money-making idea is to keep an eye out for contests and competitions that award cash prizes. Each year numerous talent contests are held to showcase a variety of abilities and interests. Earning money based around things you love is a win-win-win. You get to enjoy your hobbies and passions, earn toward your future, and add achievements to your résumé.

Next time you're tempted to spend your hard-earned dollars rather than saving them for college, remember what you're investing in and why you're making these sacrifices. The goal isn't to have to pinch pennies and work around the clock for the rest of your life, but to propel yourself into the school, career, and future of your dreams.

Crowdfunding

Maybe you have people in your life who would be willing to contribute to your college education. Today it is easier than ever for family and friends to pitch in. Websites like GoFundMe and Indiegogo have become household names, with almost everyone on social media having seen some sort of campaign cross their newsfeed. This type of crowdsourcing has now stretched into the world of education, with many popular sites having education sections in addition to the new, college-specific crowdfunding sites that are entering the scene.

Consider an alternative like this to help build your college savings in the years before you enroll. Graduation and birthdays are great opportunities to post a page announcing that any monetary gifts will go toward your schooling. While most of the students who've participated in these campaigns haven't raised enough for a full ride, many have received a few thousand dollars toward college costs. And every bit makes a difference!

Think It Through

Once you and your family have figured out how to generate additional funds for college, the next question is where to put them. As we've discussed, compound interest is a powerful tool that can multiply an investment, allowing you to save much more over time than you initially put in. You want to make sure your money is hard at work, making additional income for you!

When it comes to setting aside money for college, you and your family will also want to strategically think through the kind of impact your savings may have on your financial aid package. Any college or university you're accepted by will put this package together, which comprises all the funding you'll be offered by that school plus government sources. It's based on information you provide in the Free Application for Federal Student Aid, more commonly known as the FAFSA.

Parent and student assets can greatly affect the amount of financial aid you're offered. Therefore, learning the smartest ways to save *in your situation* can help you not only get the best return on your savings but can make you eligible for a better financial aid package.

In chapter 4, we'll discuss financial aid in more detail—including how to file your FAFSA—and learn how to best allocate income and assets.

Where to Put Your Money

There are many savings vehicles available, offering great benefits and incentives for the college-bound. As we take a look at the most popular ones, encourage your parents to read this section on their own for some additional, big-picture ideas.

529 PLANS

A 529 savings plan is specifically designed to help families set aside money for college. Any US citizen or resident alien 18 or older can open one of these accounts, designating a beneficiary (a recipient) such as a child, grandchild, or younger relative. Adults can also open one of these accounts to pay for their own educational expenses.

Setting up an automatic monthly deposit in a 529 plan is a great option for many families. There are two types of 529s: *prepaid tuition plans* and *college savings plans*.

The *prepaid tuition plans* allow you to purchase all or part of your future college credits at current costs. Your money is guaranteed to grow at the same rate as tuition. So if you pay in half of tuition at today's price, it will always be worth half of tuition—10, 20, or even 30 years from now. The burden of growth or loss falls on the state or program offering the plan, which takes the volatility of the stock market out of the equation for account holders. These plans come in many forms, with some covering only tuition and fees, and others covering all qualified higher-education expenses. There are separate 529s for private and public colleges and universities. Since the recession, the number of states specifically offering prepaid plans has dwindled; however, some still have them as an option. Get more information at Savingforcollege.com.

Nearly every state offers a *college savings plan*. According to Savingforcollege.com, these plans resemble retirement accounts in that the money you contribute gets invested in options like mutual funds, and your account value varies depending on how well your selected investment does. Tuition rates are not locked in as they are for a prepaid plan; however, a 529 plan has the potential to earn greater returns over time. Check with a financial broker or 529 plan manager about setting one up.

Advantages

- Funds grow tax-free and will not be taxed when taken out for college-related expenses
- Low maintenance: you can set up automatic payments through your bank or company payroll department, and the program manager will handle the investments

- The donor stays in control of the account and can assure money is used for its intended purpose
- High contribution limits
- Everyone is eligible regardless of income

Disadvantages

- Contributions are not federally tax deductible (state tax benefits vary depending on where you live)
- Withdrawals not used for qualified educational expenses are taxed and penalized
- The prepaid tuition plans are often limited to public in-state schools, so the beneficiary won't receive the maximum benefit if he or she elects to attend an out-of-state or private school
- Investment options are limited to pre-established portfolios set by the plan manager
- How accounts and distributions affect FAFSA varies on who the account owner is and when the distributions are made

COVERDELL EDUCATION SAVINGS ACCOUNT

The Coverdell is very similar to a 529 college savings plan, except that the contributions can also be used for qualifying elementary and secondary school expenses, and the owner has greater ability to choose how the money is invested.

Advantages

- Allows the owner more control over investment options, similar to an individual retirement account (IRA)
- Funds grow tax-free and will not be taxed when taken out for education-related expenses
- Can be used to pay for private grade school and high school expenses prior to college

Disadvantages

- Income restrictions: You must make less than $110,000 a year individually or under $220,000 as a married couple filing jointly
- Low contribution limit: $2,000 per year, per beneficiary
- The account must be set up and all contributions made before the beneficiary turns 18
- Limited parental control after student turns 18. Contributions will eventually be distributed to the beneficiary if not used for educational expenses

ROTH IRA

A lot of families choose to take advantage of a Roth IRA as their vehicle for college savings. Roths are often assumed to be exclusively for retirement, but they can also offer key benefits when used to cover college costs.

The accounts grow tax-deferred, and withdrawals are exempt from penalties if used for qualified higher-education expenses. If you invest in a Roth IRA with college funding specifically in mind, it's still very important to protect your retirement assets, ensuring you'll have the needed funds once you no longer work.

Advantages

- Flexibility: funds can be used for both educational expenses and retirement
- No penalties when withdrawals are used for educational expenses
- Earns tax-deferred interest
- Not considered an asset on the FAFSA

Disadvantages

- Annual contribution limit of $5,500 (or $6,500 for people over 50)
- Not available to high-income individuals. You must make under $116,000 a year individually or less than $183,000 as a married couple filing jointly to contribute the full amount
- Distributions for educational expenses are reported as income and could hurt a son or daughter's financial aid eligibility the following year

- Tax-free withdrawals for college expenses are limited to the actual amount contributed, and any amount above the original contribution may be taxed

For Parents: Upromise

If you frequently shop online, you may want to consider a Upromise Goal Saver account from Sallie Mae. This program offers cash back for college costs at many online retailers, as well as a credit card with cash-back incentives.

You can also contribute personal funds to the account, link it with a 529 savings plan, or track your savings goals on their platform.

ADDITIONAL OPTIONS

Don't forget there are other ways to invest your money, including:

- Interest-bearing savings accounts
- CDs and bonds
- Peer-to-peer lending
- Real estate transactions
- And more

Families and students have successfully used a variety of methods to help pay for college expenses. While each approach offers different benefits, the most important thing is that you find what works for you and commit to it. Even if you don't pick the fastest-growing option with the highest interest, committing and contributing to a steady savings plan is better than no savings at all.

Prepare Rather Than Predict

We save money because we can't predict the future. Hopefully, you'll get a full ride or be offered an incredible financial aid package. And I suppose that American higher education could even be free someday. But when it comes to your education, preparation trumps a gamble.

When you have the opportunity to stash money away, do it. Make the most of what you have today. Even if it's a small amount, those dollars *will* add up! Remember . . . you're investing in yourself, and *you are worth it*!

SUMMARY POINTS

▶ Savings advice typically falls into two broad categories: cutting back or earning more. The first takes more of a minimalistic, budget–focused approach; the second encourages the pursuit of additional income that can be deposited into savings. Your best approach depends on your personal situation.

▶ Though you can invest your college savings in various places, these options generally carry the most benefits for college-bound students and parents: 529 Plans, Coverdell Education Savings Accounts, and Roth IRAs.

▶ Make a choice and stick with it. Any amount of savings is better than none at all.

3

PRE-COLLEGE ACTIONS

Cutting Costs Before You Enroll

The secret to getting ahead is getting started.

Mark Twain

O ur calendars tend to fill up fast. The pressure of everyday life sometimes demands so much of our time that preparing for what's next gets pushed to the back burner. Let me encourage you: don't put off college prep. Taking time to do some strategic planning beforehand can make a big impact during and after college.

What can you be doing in the current moment to be ready for college and the future you dream of? Plenty! There are steps you can take well before you reach campus that will save you time, reduce stress, and drastically cut costs. Let's discuss some of those pre-college actions.

Earn Credits in Advance

Having college-level credits prior to enrolling full time is a great head start. The fewer credit hours you need to graduate equals fewer semesters to pay for, which equals big bucks saved! On average, one less semester at a private university would reduce your college costs by $21,960!

Those credits can also help if you're concerned you might need a little more time to earn that degree. Research by the National Center for Education Statistics reveals that only 40 percent of students pursuing degrees at four-year institutions beginning in 2007 graduated in four years, while 60 percent took longer or did not graduate at all. The extra time comes at a price. Earning credit before you reach college is one way to ensure you still graduate on schedule.

These advance credits can also reduce redundancies in your curriculum, which means you're less likely to get bored! It can be nice to skip English 101 in college (thanks to your AP class in high school) and move on to more specialized courses that capture your interest, like creative writing and journalism. You could also use these credits to open up free time in your schedule, allowing you to take on a lighter academic load each semester. As any college student will tell you, 12 hours is a lot more fun than 18 hours—especially if you're interested in participating in campus life!

Here are several ways to earn college credit before you step foot on campus.

AP AND IB COURSES

By enrolling in Advanced Placement (AP) and International Baccalaureate (IB) classes, you are signing up for college-level courses. At the end of these courses, you have the opportunity to complete a standardized test. If you earn high enough scores, you receive college credit that is accepted by many colleges and universities throughout the country. AP (but not IB) exams can be taken without enrolling in a course; however, courses are typically recommended, as each one is designed to help you succeed in the exam.

Beyond saving you money, these courses can also benefit your college applications. Admissions officers look on them favorably, because they demonstrate that you've chosen to challenge yourself with the most demanding coursework available. Showing this kind of drive and ambition can give you an edge on admission to more competitive schools, as well as help qualify you for more merit (or achievement-based) scholarship award dollars.

CLEP EXAMS

The College Board's CLEP (College-Level Examination Program) exams are another option for earning credits prior to enrolling. Thirty-three exams are offered in five subject areas and are accepted by more than 2,900 colleges and universities around the country. Three or more credits are awarded for each exam passed, with the number varying depending on the subject and the policies of the college you attend.

A benefit of these tests is that they don't require you to take specific classes. Instead, they assess your knowledge of a subject, regardless of how you acquired it. So even if you attended a tiny high school that doesn't offer AP or IB courses, are homeschooled, learned on the job, or studied outside the US, you can still earn college credit with the CLEP exams if you've learned the right stuff!

DUAL ENROLLMENT

Many high schools are now partnered with local colleges to offer dual enrollment classes, which allow students the opportunity to simultaneously earn high school and college credit. Some dual enrollment programs have students take these college-level courses at their high school; others require students to attend classes on the college campus. The cost of dual enrollment credits can vary between programs. Many high schools have worked out partnerships that allow students to take these classes for free or at a very low cost, while some colleges charge fees comparable to their regular tuition rates.

Should you choose to attend the partnering college once you've graduated high school, your credits will immediately transfer. However, this may not be the case if you select a different school. Due to variations in the difficulty of courses and the structure of these partnerships, dual enrollment credits are not as commonly accepted as those from AP and IB courses. Look into whether your high school offers this option and if the colleges you are considering accept this type of credit.

EARLY COLLEGE HIGH SCHOOLS

A recent and growing trend is the emergence of early college high schools. They more fully immerse students in college-level courses while simultaneously allowing them to earn a high school diploma and up to two years of college credit—tuition free.

These schools, which gear their entire curriculum toward college prep, were primarily designed to help underrepresented students increase their potential for academic success. Thus far the research has shown great results, with 94 percent of attendees earning college credit and 30 percent earning an associate's degree or other post-secondary credential while in high school. At last report, there were 280 of these schools with more than 80,000 students in attendance.

You may want to consider this alternative, especially if saving money and getting a jump-start on your college degree is a top priority.

COULD THIS BE AN OPTION FOR YOU?

Very possibly! If you can handle the course load and the time commitment, then the answer may be yes. However, take a moment to weigh the cost before jumping in.

While there are strong incentives for pursuing college credit while in high school, it's even more important to do well in your current classes and maintain a strong grade point average (GPA). Know your limits and realize it's totally acceptable to get college credits *once you're in college*. High school on its own can be a lot of pressure. You have to find the right balance for you.

At the same time, don't let fear or laziness make your choice. If earning credits in advance will make your dreams a reality, give it a shot and push yourself. Whether or not the credits transfer to your prospective college or university, earning them in advance can still benefit your future.

In high school, I completed 15 dual enrollment hours through my local community college. The courses—such as US History and Spanish—were ones that I needed to take anyway as part of my high school requirements. The school I ultimately chose to attend, Vanderbilt University, is highly competitive and did not accept these credits. Yet what some might perceive as a waste of time, I view as a huge positive. Given the opportunity, I would make the same decision all over again for a few reasons:

1. I believe being able to state that I had completed a semester's worth of college coursework reflected very positively on my college and scholarship applications. While those credit hours didn't technically end up "counting" on my college transcript, I'm convinced they made me a more competitive applicant in the admissions and scholarship process.

2. Taking these courses helped prepare me for the rigors of higher education. I went from a smaller public high school to a competitive Top 20 university. While getting used to the more difficult coursework at Vanderbilt was still a challenge, having already taken some advanced courses laid a better foundation and strengthened my confidence, enabling me to make a smoother transition.

3. It didn't take much additional effort to earn these credits. Aside from filling out a few forms and paying a relatively small fee to enroll, I took the kinds of classes I would have needed to as a high school student. And while these dual enrollment courses were slightly more challenging, I was inclined to take more difficult classes anyway so I would be prepared for college and in the best position to win scholarships.

4. I had a great backup plan in case I didn't get accepted into my dream school or earn enough scholarships to pay for it. I knew the credits would in fact transfer to

a state school, and if I ended up taking that route, I'd have a full semester already completed.

Explore the best ways for you to earn advance credit and make an informed decision. Your school counselor can tell you what's available and help evaluate your best options. Then it's up to you: go ahead and make it happen!

A Big Head Start

In high school, my friend Karen Swetland had a clear vision for accelerating her college education and was determined to reach her goal. She signed up for every AP course she could, as well as took a few dual enrollment courses. She said, "I didn't know where I was going to college, but I knew those credits would help me get into the best school [by showing what I was capable of] and let me skip ahead in college."

After high school graduation, she enrolled in the Vanderbilt University engineering program with over 38 credit hours already under her belt. Her strategic thinking continued as she devised a plan to not only complete her bachelor's degree requirements in four years but also earn her master's in the same time frame. On graduation day, while her peers were receiving one degree, she was walking away with two!

Karen admits the road wasn't easy, and tremendous determination was needed (she took 17–20 credit hours every semester and even had to convince her advisor to get on board with her plan), but she ultimately earned herself a tremendous jump-start on her career. When asked about her advice for upcoming students aspiring to follow a similar path, Karen responded, "Always look for opportunities to excel and push yourself."

Karen went on to earn a PhD and work in a highly respected engineering position for the US government in Washington, DC—all before her twenty-seventh birthday. She serves as a shining example that earning college credit in advance can give you an incredible head start on your future!

College-Prep Costs

The college application process can be surprisingly expensive. Many people are aware of the high costs of college tuition and fees, but they are caught off guard by how much money they spend simply getting accepted into the right school. Sixty-five dollars for an application fee one day, and $54 for an exam registration the next—and before you know it, you're several hundred dollars over budget . . . and you haven't even set foot on campus!

From test and application fees to travel costs for college tours, it's easy to spend way more money than anticipated, quickly squeezing a tight budget. Fortunately, there are ways to help offset some of these expenses. A bit of work and initiative may be required, but they can make a big difference over time and enable you to apply for multiple colleges without stressing about the costs.

SAVE ON STANDARDIZED TESTS

If you're anywhere near the time to start applying for college, you've likely heard quite a bit about standardized tests like the ACT and SAT. Colleges and universities use these exams to evaluate students for admission. Nearly every college-bound student will take one or both of these tests. There are also several others you may be required or elect to take, such as:

- The PSAT
- The PLAN (a practice exam for the ACT)
- AP exams
- CLEP exams
- SAT IIs (or SAT subject tests)
- The TOEFL (an English-proficiency exam for non-native English speakers)
- Other state-specific exams

Except for state-required exams, these tests aren't free! It's very common for students to take the SAT or ACT multiple times until they achieve their desired score, which means not only do they pay the first time around but every time they retake one. Plus, many students take multiple AP, CLEP, or SAT II subject tests as well. Considering that registration for the SAT is $54.50, and each AP exam costs $92, taking the SAT three times and testing for three to five AP classes would cost between $440 and $624! And that doesn't even include what many families shell out in order to ready their kids for these tests, such as hiring private tutors and enrolling them in expensive prep courses. Factor that all together, and you see how the expenses can really start to pile up.

With college tuition and fees just around the corner, these add-ons are simply overwhelming to many students and their families. Let's discuss a few ways to help curb any unnecessary spending.

Pick the Right Test

Colleges allow applicants to choose between entrance exams. While you may be inclined to take both the ACT and the SAT and see where you do best, being selective has its advantages: you can focus your efforts on preparing for one exam and cut down on test fees.

However, don't choose simply because your school counselor is more familiar with the SAT, or because you've heard your friends talk about the ACT. There is plenty of information about these tests both online and in book form to help you make a knowledgeable decision. You can even go so far as to take practice tests to see which one you tend to score best on. Because the two exams test the subject matter in different ways, you may find that one plays more to your strengths. Really explore how each one works, and then make an informed choice.

Nearly half of all states—and individual school districts in many others—now require that either the ACT or SAT be administered to high school students. If a specific test is mandated, the state or school district will foot the bill. This means that residents have the opportunity to take it at least once for free. If you feel that particular exam is worth another try—or you've determined the other test is a better fit—you will have to pay the fee the second time around, but you're also getting two tries for the price of one!

Students who are particularly keen on being admitted to a top college or university may want to attempt each test at least once for the best shot at a high score. While students generally perform similarly well on these tests, you won't know with 100 percent certainty without trying both. There isn't any harm in exercising your options if you have the time and resources to invest. But if you're intent on saving money on registration fees, carefully focusing your efforts on one exam can be a smart move.

Test Fee Waivers

SAT or ACT fee waivers are available to high school juniors and seniors who meet one or more of the following criteria:

- Enrolled in the Federal Free or Reduced Price Lunch Program at school
- Enrolled in certain programs for students from low-income families (example: Upward Bound)
- Lives in a foster home, is a ward of the state, or is homeless
- Family receives public assistance or lives in government-subsidized housing
- Family's annual income falls within USDA Income Eligibility Guidelines

The sponsoring organizations make their exams free for these qualified students.

To obtain a fee waiver, visit your school counselor. He or she will verify your eligibility and administer the waiver. Homeschooled students may obtain vouchers through a local public high school counselor.

Because counselors must go through a verification process on your behalf, be sure to allow ample time prior to your test date for your fee waiver to be obtained. Once you're deemed eligible, you can receive up to four SAT fee waivers, which cover the registration costs of two SAT exams as well as two SAT subject tests. For the ACT exam, eligible students can receive up to two fee waivers.

Both the SAT and the ACT waivers also cover the cost of up to four score reports, meaning that your test results will get sent to any four colleges or universities of your choice for free.

Here are a few additional money-saving tips for standardized testing:

▸ Register on time to prevent late fees. While a $28 penalty may not seem like much, it's completely avoidable. Considering the abundance of fees surrounding college admission, don't let extra costs like this derail your budget.

▸ Explore inexpensive test-prep options, including:

- Free online tutorials such as those offered by Khan Academy
- Various smartphone apps that offer free or low-cost test prep
- Test-prep classes offered by your school
- SAT or ACT study groups
- Sample questions and practice tests on the College Board's SAT website

▸ If your state or district makes it available, take advantage of SAT School Day. This gives you the opportunity to take the test for free during school hours.

Skip the Tests Altogether

You may be surprised to learn that more than 800 four-year colleges and universities do not require students to submit standardized test scores. Instead, these test-optional (or test-flexible) colleges place a greater emphasis on other aspects of the college application such as your GPA, class rank, extra-curricular activities, letters of recommendation, and essays. Among these "flexible" colleges are several prestigious institutions including Wake Forest University, Bates College, and Wesleyan University. A full list of schools is available online at FairTest.org.

If you know *with certainty* that your prospective colleges are test-optional, it is possible to skip standardized entrance exams all together, presuming that your state allows it. Of course, that's a big decision that can limit you should you change your mind at the last minute. Therefore, weigh all aspects of the decision carefully.

SAVE ON COLLEGE APPLICATIONS

Admissions experts typically recommend that students apply for between five and eight colleges, though a significant number of students apply to 10 or more. According to a *US News & World Report* survey of nearly 1,100 ranked colleges, the average application fee is $41. As you can imagine, these fees can accumulate rapidly. If possible, reduce your costs by obtaining fee waivers, which allow you to apply for free.

There are several options for getting application fees

waived, and they generally only take a few minutes of your time. I'll break them down into four main categories:

- Fee waivers based on financial need
- Fee waivers based on merit
- Fee waivers based on expressed interest
- Miscellaneous fee waivers

Don't let the technical terminology on some of these throw you. I'll explain them all now.

Fee Waivers Based on Financial Need
The most common application fee waiver is based on financial need, and a number of qualifiers include:

- Eligible for the Federal Free or Reduced Price Lunch Program
- Eligible for, or has received, an SAT or ACT fee waiver
- Family income falls within the Income Eligibility Guidelines established by the USDA Food and Nutrition Service
- Family receives public assistance
- Living in federally subsidized housing, a foster home, or is homeless
- Student is a ward of the state or an orphan

You can obtain these waivers through three sources: the National Association of College Admissions Counselors (NACAC), the College Board, or the college or university where you plan to apply. Typically the NACAC waiver is secured through your high school counselor. However, if he or she doesn't have the form, it can be downloaded from the NACAC website. Students can use the NACAC form for up to four schools.

Those who received a fee waiver for their SAT are automatically qualified for four college application fee waivers through the College Board. Eligible seniors get these waivers when they obtain their SAT score, and juniors will receive them in the fall of their senior year. Not all colleges accept the waivers, but many do. You can browse a list of those schools on the College Board's Big Future website. The NACAC does not currently maintain a directory of participating schools, so if you are eligible, contact the Office of Admission at your top-choice colleges to learn if the waiver is accepted.

And keep this in mind: because the NACAC and the College Board are separate entities, eligible students can use fee waivers from both programs, enabling them to apply to up to eight colleges free of charge! Beyond this, some schools themselves will waive a student's application fees based on financial criteria. Review the website or call the admissions office of colleges you're interested in to see whether this is something they offer.

Fee Waivers Based on Merit

Academically strong and/or highly involved students may be able to receive fee waivers. Colleges want to attract the best and brightest each year, and if forgoing a $50 application fee helps top scholars pick them, then it's a simple sacrifice to make. Some schools offer fee waivers for National Merit, National Achievement, or National Hispanic finalists. Other schools make them available to students with a certain GPA or test score. If you are an especially accomplished student and want to save some money on college application fees, peruse the websites of the schools you're interested in or call their admissions offices about these waivers.

Fee Waivers Based on Expressed Interest

Basically, *expressed interest* is demonstrated when students show they are intent on applying to a specific college or university—either by visiting a campus, attending a college fair, or participating in certain campus programs. When you tour a school or meet with an admissions representative at a fair, an application fee waiver is sometimes included in the packet they give you. College recruiters will also often pass out codes or special forms that you can use to waive the application fee.

Miscellaneous Fee Waivers

In the broad miscellaneous category, there are a variety of

other, less-specific reasons that colleges may offer application fee waivers. A few of these are:

- *Service activities.* Performing a certain number of service hours or being an alumnus of a service-based group like AmeriCorps or the Peace Corps may qualify you. Typically, these fee waivers are available to older students seeking admission versus teens right out of high school. Check with the schools you're interested in about this.

- *Applying early.* Students can apply for college in various time frames, most commonly referred to as Early Decision, Early Action, and Regular Decision. For those who choose Early Decision, they get to submit their college applications ahead of their peers, but they also make a binding commitment to attend that school if accepted. Early Action students also have the advantage of applying in advance, but they are not bound to attend a particular school. Some colleges look favorably upon Early applicants (of either type), waiving their fees as an incentive to apply prior to Regular Decision applicants.

- *College employee, veteran, or child of a veteran.* Employees of a college or their dependents may qualify for a waiver at that particular school. For example, 23 schools within the California State University system waive application fees for employees, and in some cases, for their spouses, domestic partners, or children as well. Veterans and children of veterans are also eligible for fee waivers at many colleges. If you fit the criteria, make sure to explore these possibilities.

- *Applying online.* An increasing number of schools offer reduced application fees, or waive fees altogether, for online applications. When browsing a university's admissions website, keep an eye out for this opportunity to save. Schools often promote it if the online application is free.

- *Special circumstances.* If your family recently experienced a major hardship or drop in finances, you may qualify. For example, a job loss, a medical emergency, the recent death of a family member, or other personal struggles may prevent you from being able to afford college application fees. In these exceptional situations, some schools will offer a waiver as long as you report and document your circumstance. Inquire with the college's or university's admissions office.

SAVE ON CAMPUS TOURS
AND COLLEGE VISITS

In the US alone, there are nearly 5,000 accredited schools of higher learning. From liberal arts colleges in small towns to huge universities in big cities, and from conservative, community-focused cultures to more eclectic, fast-paced environments, your choices are practically endless. That's one of the wonderful things about applying for college in America: you have the opportunity to select a school that fits *you*!

In case having that many choices feels a bit stressful, campus tours are a great way to both narrow the options and help ensure you find a college that feels like a home away from home. The problem is in the cost, especially if you're looking out of state. Let's discuss a few strategies to help you get a good look at schools without breaking the bank.

Virtual College Tours

These tours, which allow you to "see" a college campus for free online, make it possible to get an in-depth visual without actually having to pack your bags. You can find these tours on many school websites, or through platforms such as CampusTours.com and Youvisit.com. While ultimately there may still be a few places you want to visit in person, virtual tours can help you exclude all but the ones with the best potential for you.

College Fairs

These events bring together college admissions representatives from multiple schools to speak with prospective students and answer any questions. While this method doesn't allow you to walk the campus, meeting with these ambassadors can still provide you with a great overview and a lot of information about a college without any cost to you. Plus, you can get to know many schools within a few hours—all in one place!

Many colleges also send representatives directly to high schools at some point during the academic year. Check with your school counselor for a list of dates and times when campus representatives may be visiting your community or region, and for information on nearby college fairs. You can also visit the NACAC's website for a list of their major regional fairs.

Fly-In Programs

Some colleges offer fly-in programs, which allow you to travel to the campus for a visit, with expenses (round-trip transportation, lodging, and possibly even meals) paid. The majority of these opportunities are extended through recruitment initiatives for targeted high school seniors—most often first-generation college students, minorities, low-income students, or underrepresented groups such as females in STEM (Science, Technology, Engineering, and Math) programs. Designed to let you briefly see what it's like to actually attend the college, these programs typically pack the visits with activities and information sessions.

Similar to the regular admissions process, fly-in programs are usually very competitive and require students to fill out an application proving their merit and eligibility. Colleges are seeking targeted applicants who have already excelled in academics and/or extracurricular activities, as well as up-and-comers they can encourage to succeed in spite of limited resources. Finding fly-ins may require a bit of research, but they can be a great opportunity for qualifying students.

Reimbursements

You may be able to earn back your campus-visit investment through reimbursements or earned tuition credits. Some schools offer travel reimbursements to long-distance applicants. Others will apply the expenses from your campus visit toward future tuition costs if you end up attending their school. Explore this option wherever you tour, and remember to document your trip expenses, just in case.

Smart Planning

If you're interested in attending college in a particular region, plan to see multiple campuses at one time rather than making separate trips. Also, check the school websites to see if they offer discounted meals and hotels for visiting students. See chapter 9 for some tips on budgeting and cutting travel costs. A few extra hours of planning can save you hundreds of dollars on college tours.

Running the Marathon

Think of paying for college as a marathon. By maintaining a steady stride between spending and saving, you can make it through each leg of the race and cross the finish line debt-free. It can be easy to get caught up in the rush of preparing for college and not even realize how all those seemingly inconsequential fees and expenses are exhausting your budget. But being mindful of the ways you can save will keep you from burning out and falling short of your goal. The more you're able to save up front, the more you'll have available to put toward the larger expenses that are coming, such as college tuition. So keep up the pace—every dollar you save puts you one step closer to your #notgoingbroke dreams.

SUMMARY POINTS

- Students can earn college credits in advance through AP and IB courses, CLEP exams, dual enrollment, and early college high schools.

- Save on college entrance exams using strategies such as selecting the right test for you, test fee waivers, or applying to test-optional colleges.

- College application fee waivers are available based on: financial need, merit, expressed interest, and other miscellaneous reasons.

▶ Cut back on the cost of college tours by utilizing virtual options, college fairs, fly-in programs, reimbursements, and smart planning.

FINANCIAL AID

Dollars & Sense

Have no fear of moving into the unknown.

Pope John Paul II

A College Board survey reported that in 2015–16 the average cost of attending a public, in-state university was more than $19,500, and a private university cost just shy of $44,000. Thankfully, most families will not have to pay full price.

According to the US Department of Education, over 80 percent of full-time undergraduates receive some form of financial aid, and about two-thirds pay for college with the help of grants and scholarships. For the 2014–15 school year, the College Board says those full-time students received an average of $14,210 in assistance.

Taking the time to understand how financial aid works is extremely important and can lead to big rewards. Don't be overwhelmed by all the forms, terms, and acronyms.

Together, we are going to learn what it takes to maximize your financial aid and get you closer to funding your college dreams!

FAFSA

Both the government and schools themselves offer most students assistance based on their financial need. To determine your need, the US Department of Education has the FAFSA (Free Application for Federal Student Aid), which you will fill out prior to your first year of college, as well as each year you are enrolled. This form asks a lot of questions about your family's finances, including how much you and your parents earn and what kind of assets you have. Your information is then plugged into the department's formula to generate your Expected Family Contribution, or EFC. The EFC is the amount of money the government believes your family should be able to contribute toward your college education. *Visit FAFSA.ed.gov and use the FAFSA4caster tool to get an idea of what your EFC will be.*

What Makes You Independent?

You will file the FAFSA as either a dependent or independent student. In high school, I initially thought I might qualify as an independent student because I was responsible for funding my own education. But I learned that "independent" has a different definition in the financial aid world.

With a few exceptions, most first-time college students are classified as dependents regardless of the relationship they have with their parents, and whether or not their parents are contributing toward their education. Dependent students must enter their parents' financial information, not just their own.

If your parents are separated or divorced, the financial information of the one you lived with the most or who assisted you the most financially over the past year is used. Typically, this is the parent who claimed you as a dependent on their taxes.

Independent students enter only their own financial information unless they are married. You are automatically considered independent if you meet one of the following criteria:

- At least 24 years old
- Married or separated (but not divorced)
- Will be enrolled in a master's or doctoral program
- Are a veteran or currently serving on active duty in the armed forces for a purpose other than training
- Have a child or dependent who receives more than half of his or her support from you
- At any time since the age of 13 have been in foster care, were a ward of the court, or both your parents were deceased
- Are an emancipated minor or in a legal guardianship as determined by a court
- Are homeless or at risk of homelessness as determined by the director of a HUD-approved homeless shelter, transitional program, or high school liaison

FILLING OUT THE FAFSA

When completing the FAFSA form, you will be asked to identify which prospective colleges you would like your paperwork sent to. This information goes to each school's financial aid department, which uses your FAFSA-generated Expected Family Contribution to create a financial aid package. This package details the financial assistance that the government and the school will offer you based on the cost of attendance, or COA. The COA tallies tuition, fees, room and board, books, and any other expenses a student accrues *as a student* at that campus. The options in the financial aid package come from a variety of places, including loans, grants, work-study programs, and scholarships.

Your FAFSA can be completed by paper or online; however, the online process is much easier and offers system checks that minimize errors. Before sitting down to fill out the form, make sure you and a parent have applied for an FSA (Federal Student Aid) ID. You can do this through the FAFSA section on the US Department of Education's website by entering personal and login information. The ID is required to access the FAFSA form and to sign the accompanying legal documents. Because the ID is basically your electronic signature, take care to keep it confidential.

You should also have access to your key financial information, as it will be necessary for filling out the FAFSA.

It's helpful to have your taxes completed and your return on hand, since a lot of the information is the same. You may be eligible to use the IRS Data Retrieval Tool, which further saves time by automatically pre-filling much of the FAFSA with your tax information. (It also decreases the chances of your FAFSA being selected for verification, which is something like an IRS audit.)

And here's some good news for you: filing the FAFSA is usually simpler than people think. WhiteHouse.gov states, "Today students and families on average fill out the FAFSA in about 20 minutes, only one third of the time it took seven years ago." So, as important as it is to get it done, it's also not something to dread. Just be intentional about completing it early and accurately, so you can get on to the more exciting parts of college planning.

CSS Profile and Other College-Specific Forms

Some colleges and scholarship programs also have students fill out the College Board's CSS/Financial Aid PROFILE®, along with university-specific financial aid forms, to determine need and the aid package offered. The CSS PROFILE is an online form that supplies requesting institutions with additional financial information to help determine eligibility for private, non-federal assistance. If your college requires this form as well, visit css.collegeboard.org for more information.

FAFSA CHANGES FOR THE 2017–18 SCHOOL YEAR

The FAFSA is undergoing significant changes for the 2017–18 school year, with the goal of making the process more convenient for students and parents. In the past, the FAFSA became available each January 1, and the financial information provided was based on the previous year's taxes. That timeline posed a few challenges, as it was too early for a lot of families to be able to file their taxes, and too late for many students to know what their EFC would be before applying for schools in the fall.

The new FAFSA has two key changes:

1. *Earlier Financial Information.* As it stands at the time of this writing, the FAFSA is based on your "prior year," which means that if you plan to enroll in college in the fall of 2016, your family's finances from 2015 will be what's considered. With the new form, the calculations will be based on your finances from the "prior prior year," which means that if you plan to enroll in college in the fall of 2017, the FAFSA will be based on your finances from 2015. This enables families to complete their taxes before the FAFSA is available and make use of the efficient IRS Data Retrieval tool. It also saves college administrators thousands of hours, as it reduces the need for extensive verification.

2. *Earlier Submission.* The FAFSA will now be available three months earlier—nearly a year before the new school year starts. Therefore, if you plan to enroll in the fall of 2017, the FAFSA will open on October 1, 2016, rather than January 1, 2017. Being able to access the form sooner will give students more time to gather the needed information as well as learn what their EFC will be earlier on in the application process.

When a Student Is Attending College (School Year)	When a Student Can Submit a FAFSA	Which Year's Income Information Is Required
July 1, 2015–June 30, 2016	January 1, 2015–June 30, 2016	2014
July 1, 2016–June 30, 2017	January 1, 2016–June 30, 2017	2015
July 1, 2017–June 30, 2018	October 1, 2016–June 30, 2018	2015
July 1, 2018–June 30, 2019	October 1, 2017–June 30, 2019	2016

Source: http://financialaidtoolkit.ed.gov/resources/fafsa-changes-17-18-faq.pdf

TOP FAFSA FILING TIPS

Be Proactive!

It's really important to get your FAFSA turned in quickly. Some financial aid is awarded on a first-come, first-serve basis; therefore, submitting your FAFSA is your ticket to get in line. And the sooner you submit it, the closer to the front of the line you'll be. Also, the deadlines for college, state, and private aid are sometimes much earlier than the federal

FAFSA deadline. Therefore, the ideal time to file the FAFSA is as close as possible to the date it becomes available.

Be Prepared

Have your information ready—including your FSA ID, tax information, and any other relevant financial forms—prior to sitting down to complete the FAFSA. Filling out the form can be a relatively painless process, especially if you're organized.

Take Advantage of Free Resources

You don't have to look far for free information on completing your FAFSA. The Office of Federal Student Aid provides various online tools and resources. College-prep websites like Khan Academy and Edvisors offer videos and tutorials to help guide you. Even a simple online search of your specific question will often yield very effective results. Also, many high schools and communities host free FAFSA seminars and prep sessions, and CollegeGoalSundayUSA.org offers FAFSA guidance at events across the country. Speak with your school counselor to learn what's happening in your area.

Follow Deadlines

Calendar and track critical FAFSA due dates. Beyond the overall federal deadline, there are also state and school-specific deadlines that may fall much earlier. Federal and state FAFSA deadlines are non-negotiable. I've heard horror stories of students missing out on renewing major grants because they missed a due date by just a few days. Get all your documents together and set reminders in your phone or computer to make sure you stay on top of your application deadlines.

Ask for Help

If you hit a point that feels confusing to you, don't hesitate to reach out to someone who can guide you through. It's better to admit you're struggling a little and get some advice than to possibly enter the wrong information or miss out on aid dollars. I promise you, this process feels overwhelming for a lot of people, and there's no shame in seeking further assistance.

Explore the Options

You may be convinced that your family makes too much money to qualify for assistance, but don't be so sure! It is possible for families with more than $150,000 in annual income to receive financial aid. While it's not all "free" money (you may be offered low-interest loans, for example), you want to make sure you keep all possible doors open. And applying for financial aid makes that happen. So explore the options before you opt out. It never hurts to try. Applying for assistance can only help—and you may actually be pleasantly surprised.

Some of you may use the FAFSA calculator and be disappointed in the EFC numbers. It can be frustrating to see that your family makes more than what the formula deems as "needing aid," but don't be disheartened. There are many additional strategies we will discuss in this book to keep you moving forward, in the direction of your goal: graduating debt-free.

Elements of the Financial Aid Package

Once a university accepts you, you'll receive a letter from its financial aid office with your itemized award package. No two schools will present you with the same aid configuration, because no two schools are alike. This makes it even more important to understand the distinction between each included element.

Don't assume the final amount a school is offering comes without a cost. Parts of it may have to be paid back, or you may be required to work on campus for a portion of the money promised. So before you make the leap, look carefully at each line item in your personal financial aid package from each school.

Let's discuss those items here. Typically, the elements of a financial aid package are scholarships and grants, student loans, and work-study programs.

SCHOLARSHIPS AND GRANTS

The terms *scholarship* and *grant* are often used interchangeably to describe money that is gifted to a student with no expectation of repayment. This is clearly the most attractive form of financial aid because it's basically free money.

Most grants are distributed based on financial need as determined by one's FAFSA application. Scholarships derive from a variety of sources: some are awarded simply in response to the information you share in your admissions application; others take a bit more work, requiring you to submit additional applications, essays, and interviews. See chapter 5 for more on earning scholarships.

STUDENT LOANS

Let me tell you upfront . . . student loans stink! Once you graduate, they are like creatures that can haunt you for years and suck the joy out of your newfound success. Avoid them by all means possible!

Your financial aid package will likely contain one or more options to borrow money. Like any other kind of loan, this is money that has to be repaid, with interest. By the time you've paid off the original debt plus its compound interest, the total cost can be excessive. We'll talk more about these types of loans and how to navigate debt in chapter 7.

WORK-STUDY

Students demonstrating financial need are often offered a work-study option as part of their package. Work-study is essentially a part-time job that allows you to earn up to the fixed amount of money stated in your financial aid award letter. How much you'll be able to make depends on your level of need, your school's funding, and the number of hours you put in on the job.

Unlike income from a regular job, the money made from a work-study position will not count against you on the FAFSA. These positions could be on or off campus depending on what opportunities your school has available. See chapter 6 for more information on working while in college.

Understanding the unique financial aid award package you're offered by each school is critical. Don't simply be impressed at the overall figure; look into every element. Be sure to take into account the difference in the types of aid being extended (scholarships and grants, loans, and work-study) and calculate what your net costs will be. How much of that money will be gifted to you, and how much has to be paid back? Remember, the bottom line may seem generous, but it's important to weigh the actual cost—what you will be obligated to pay (and pay back) at each school—before finally deciding where to attend.

Know Your FAO

The financial aid office is generally among a family's first contact points with a college. Its personnel not only manage financial assistance and work-study for students but play a very important role in the scholarship process, acting as liaisons between you and any financial organization that will be disbursing funds for your education. Their staff also ensures that your money goes to the right place at the right time. Therefore, make a point to get to know the financial aid officer (FAO) assigned to you.

If you plan to pursue outside scholarship dollars, be sure to talk to an FAO at each school about how your winnings will impact your overall aid package. Each college individually determines which portion of your offer to reduce or replace with these additional funds, and the decision can vary from school to school. Some use outside scholarships to replace loans, which is ideal. Others, however, will use them to reduce the amount of grant money or school-specific scholarships you're being extended, meaning that even with the outside awards, you would still owe the same amount to attend this college. Clarifying how outside scholarships will affect your aid package and the ultimate cost at each school will help guide your choices.

Once you've finally made your decision and enrolled, you may be ready to quit thinking about financial aid and move on with college life. But it is important to maintain the relationship with your FAO and continue to monitor your funds to ensure that they all land in the right place. Failing to stay on top of this one area can cost your family thousands of dollars without you ever knowing it.

I gently battled my financial aid officers a few times regarding small errors in my package. For example, in my freshman year of college, a computer removed $1,500 from one of my scholarships and replaced that free money with a loan. Initially, my FAO didn't agree that there was a mistake. But because I had studied and understood every element of my package, I was able to explain it to her effectively, and the school reinstated the scholarship money.

The financial aid department at each college or university deals with hundreds, if not tens of thousands, of students every year and juggles millions of dollars. Mistakes can be made. Be smart, be vigilant, but of course, always be nice.

Reach!

Many students mistakenly think they could never afford to attend a top university. They simply don't realize the incredible amount of financial aid that some of the elite institutions provide.

If you have prepared yourself to be admitted to a university and have demonstrated significant financial need (as determined by your EFC), many private colleges and universities have the endowments and funding necessary to meet your need.

Because of the additional gift aid these schools typically have available, it can actually—and surprisingly—be cheaper for low-income students to go to an expensive private university than a public university. For example, you may be offered only government grants and loans at the public university, whereas the private university may have more private grants and scholarships to give away.

In fact, in seeking to attract the best and brightest, about six dozen colleges and universities (including many of the nation's most prestigious institutions) have actually implemented "no loans" financial aid policies to cover costs beyond an applicant's EFC. This means that loans are not included in one's financial aid award; only grants and work-study are offered. Some schools make this available exclusively to low-income students, while others extend it to all students, regardless of income level.

So don't limit your search to public and community colleges in "your price range" without investigating next-level possibilities. You may just find the school of your dreams at the price of your dreams.

Special Circumstances

Life isn't always predictable. Sometimes unforeseen events occur that drastically change a student's financial picture after he or she has already filed the FAFSA. Thankfully, the government allows the Office of Financial Aid at each college to recalculate a student's financial need when special circumstances arise. The criteria is limited, and considered on a case-by-case basis, but it includes situations like excessive medical bills, significant drops in income, divorce, or the death of a parent.

If you find yourself in need of a recalculation, contact your college about their process for a special-circumstances appeal. Many will require written documentation and third-party confirmation of your situation, but don't hesitate to pursue it. The worst they can say is no, and, best-case scenario, you'll be offered an aid package more in line with your current financial position.

Maximize Your Financial Aid

Navigating financial aid can sometimes feel like trying to drive across the country without a GPS: you have a general idea of the direction you're supposed to go, but figuring out the optimal route to get there is another story.

Everyone wants to get the best financial aid package possible, but it can be hard knowing which factors make the difference. You may have heard of situations where two families with seemingly similar income and assets were offered different aid packages, one getting various grants and the other walking away with only loans. So what gives?

While income generally has the biggest impact on how much financial assistance you receive, there are some additional things to pay attention to—and do—to increase your chances of getting the best aid award possible. While everyone's journey is different, having a solid road map can help you maximize your results. Here are a few strategies for navigating financial aid:

THINK AHEAD

Many students and parents assume that colleges don't pay attention to household or individual finances until a student is about to go to school. Not true. Currently, the FAFSA is calculated using your family's finances from the year prior to your enrollment. With the new FAFSA filing changes for the 2017–18 school year, the "base year" will now be two years prior. Since the financial transactions you make in a base year can drastically impact your overall award package, the goal is to be smart with your money:

1. Strategically allocate your income and assets.
2. Avoid financial decisions that could jeopardize or diminish your aid offer.

There are plenty of legitimate ways to do this. For example: rather than leaving $10,000 sitting in a savings account at year's end, perhaps your parents could pay off a credit card balance or car loan. Or they could invest that money in retirement savings, which in most cases doesn't count against the FAFSA. Also, if your family is thinking about selling an investment, they may want to wait until after the critical base years, since the formula calculates investment profits as income.

To understand how your financial decisions in years prior to filing your FAFSA will impact the outcome of your aid offer, I recommend the book *Filing the FAFSA* by Mark Kantrowitz and David Levy.

SAVE WISELY

Be strategic about where you invest your money. A dollar saved by a parent and a dollar saved by a student is viewed differently on the FAFSA. In fact, parental assets are assessed in the federal financial aid formula at no more than 5.64 percent, whereas student assets (whether dependent or independent) are assessed at 20 percent. So for a savings account with $10,000 in a parent's name, the government will expect only 5.64 percent, or $564, of that to go toward college. On the other hand, if that money is saved in a son's or daughter's savings account, it could be assessed at 20 percent, resulting in a $2,000 increase in EFC. In addition, a portion of parental assets may be protected in the EFC formula. The amount of the Asset Protection Allowance (APA) is based on the age of the oldest parent and whether or not your parents are married. However, there is no allowance for assets of dependent students. So if you're trying to decide whether to set up a savings account in a parent's name or yours, the parent's account is typically a safer bet.

There is some allowance for independent student assets, which is calculated using the same APA formula as parents, but anything over that amount will be factored at 20 percent. It should be noted that independent students as well as parents of dependent students with a combined income below $50,000 who meet certain criteria qualify for a simplified version of the FAFSA that does not factor in assets. Check the FAFSA website to find out if you're eligible.

BE MINDFUL OF YOUR INCOME

Like with assets, income is factored differently depending on whether you're a student or a parent. Eligible student income is assessed at 50 percent, regardless of dependent or independent status, while a parent's income assessment ranges between 22 and 47 percent. Also, the income protection allowance, or amount of income that is protected in the

FAFSA formula, is much higher for parents than for students. Currently, dependent students can make up to $6,400 before it is counted on the FAFSA, whereas parent income allowances vary from around $15,000 up to $38,000 based on the number of members in the household and how many are enrolled in college. Independent student income allowances start at $9,960 and range upward based on the number of dependents in the student's household.

The percentage of the parent's eligible income used to factor the EFC generally increases as overall income increases. Therefore, it is important to be aware of what will be ruled as income during base years. Capital gains distributions, withdrawals from retirement accounts, and bonuses can all be included and decrease financial aid eligibility. Be strategic about when and how these funds are allocated.

Another area that can greatly affect student income is when a non-parent (such as a grandparent or family friend) wants to contribute to your education. This could be in the form of a gift, paying for tuition, or setting up a 529 plan with you as the beneficiary. How these funds are distributed matters! Funds going directly to a student are counted as student income and can decrease your financial aid eligibility in future years by up to 50 percent of the gifted amount. If you're depending on financial aid each year to pay for school, that's a major hit! Therefore, anyone who'd like to give money directly to you, the student, or pay for your education directly on your behalf may want to instead consider:

- gifting the money to one of your parents or contributing to a parent's 529 account, or
- waiting until your junior year of college—once you are past the need for FAFSA—and then offering to help pay back any student loan debt you may have acquired.

STAY CONSISTENT

Unfortunately, just one year of strategically watching your finances doesn't cut it. Students must re-apply for the FAFSA each year they are in college. You'll want to maintain strategies to maximize financial aid through the end of the last base year.

With these tips in mind, use the FAFSA4caster early on to get an idea of what your aid eligibility and package will look like. Play around with different scenarios to better understand how the calculations work and how different factors such as extra savings and income affect the bottom line.

Keep in mind that it is a federal calculator, which means

it doesn't include monies you may receive from your college and/or state. It will, however, give you a better idea of your Expected Family Contribution, which in turn will help you more accurately anticipate what your overall package might be and the strategies you can employ to improve it.

While we cover a lot of territory in this book, there's additional information out there that you may find useful. Books like *Filing the FAFSA* by Kantrowitz and Levy go into extensive detail on each section of the form and how to best prepare for filing. Take time to learn about the details that can help you maximize your financial aid. Then use this knowledge to make a game plan so that when it's time to fill out the FAFSA, you've put yourself in the best position possible.

Tell the Truth

While several strategies can be employed to increase your financial aid eligibility, it's vital to tell the truth and not get involved in any gray areas. There's a difference between learning how to avoid hurting your eligibility within the financial aid formula, and lying about income and assets. With the system of checks and balances that are built into the financial aid process these days, dishonesty is often caught and carries serious consequences. Don't go there.

Breathe Easy

You don't have to be a financial guru or professional mathematician to navigate financial aid and file the FAFSA with ease. Just take it one step at a time. Be intentional with each financial decision you make, keeping in mind how it will affect your aid package in the future.

And don't worry if you're unsure or don't understand everything right away. With all the resources available, the answers should be easily within your reach. In the long run, the more you learn about your financial picture, the better off you'll be, not just with financial aid, but in the bigger world beyond college!

Now take a deep breath and let the information soak in. I know it's a lot to process, but rest assured: you've got this!

SUMMARY POINTS

▶ College-bound students must fill out a FAFSA to be eligible for financial aid. The formula used through this form generates an Expected Family Contribution, which is the amount the government believes you and your parents should be able to pay toward your education.

▶ A few key tips for filing the FAFSA include: be proactive, be prepared, take advantage of free resources, and follow deadlines.

- The FAFSA will be undergoing significant changes for the 2017–18 school year, requiring students to provide financial information from an earlier year and allowing for submission three months sooner.

- The elements of a financial aid package are scholarships and grants, student loans, and work-study. Become familiar with each element and seek to understand the package you are offered. You are your own best advocate in this process.

- Many top colleges offer significant amounts of gift aid to low-income students, sometimes making it cheaper for high-need students to attend private institutions over public universities.

- In the EFC equation, student income and assets are factored at a significantly higher percentage than that of their parents.

- To maximize your financial aid, don't forget to think ahead, save wisely, be mindful of your income, and stay consistent.

5

SCHOLARSHIPS
Free Money for College

Knowing is not enough; we must apply.
Being willing is not enough; we must do.
Leonardo da Vinci

When I close my eyes, I can still see it: that big, white envelope crammed into the tiny mailbox on our front porch. I knew what it was; it was an answer. A yes or a no to whether my college dreams would come true.

For weeks I had been tirelessly submitting scholarship application after scholarship application, praying something would come through. A few days earlier, I had gathered the family around and excitedly ripped open a similar letter only to find . . . I was rejected. So in that moment, as I worked to free the envelope from our mailbox, I was torn between hopefulness and frustration. Feeling pressured by a big project due the next day, and worn out by midterms, cross-country practice, and a long night at work, I immediately thought, *I'm not sure I can take another rejection letter right now!* Still, I noticed, *That last letter was smaller. Maybe this time is different.*

Holding my breath, I tore open the crisp, white paper . . . *"You've been selected!"*

I read the words over and over through tears of joy.

I was scared it might be a fluke until several other large envelopes containing acceptance letters arrived. Soon, over $500,000 in scholarship award letters came through, and I had more money than I needed for college!

My dream had become real.

You Can Too!

According to Debt.org, over $46 billion in grant and scholarship dollars is given away each year by the US Department of Education and America's colleges and universities. Beyond that, private sources gift well over another $3 billion. So the money is there—and it's free! Why not go after your share?

With most scholarship programs, you are awarded a sizable sum of money with few or no strings attached, making scholarships the ideal way to pay for college. And while filling out several pages of information for each application may seem tedious on the front end, it's time well spent, considering that it can lead to thousands of dollars in savings.

Don't have perfect grades? Not a star athlete? That's okay! When I started my scholarship journey, I felt completely inadequate for the challenge. I was a freshman in high school and didn't feel like much of a standout. But when my mom told me I would have to come up with the funds myself, I became really intent on figuring out what made an applicant successful and how I could set myself apart from the crowd. I read countless books and articles on the topic and interviewed alumni who had been winners in the scholarship process. I then came up with a plan and was determined to make it work.

I challenge you to find that same drive within yourself. Too many students forgo scholarships altogether or give the process only a halfhearted effort because they're afraid of being rejected. I encourage you to face your fears and apply anyway!

When I interviewed other scholarship winners for my first book, one thing nearly all of us had in common was rejection. For every scholarship we won, several more turned us down. To one scholarship program, we were the ideal candidates; to another, someone else was a better fit. Yet we all still won full rides and graduated debt-free because we kept pushing and didn't let rejection shake our confidence. In fact, a friend of mine received nothing but rejection letters for the first eight months he spent applying for scholarships. Then one week he received two full-ride offers in a row. Enduring the few months of disappointment was completely worth the ultimate win of a debt-free education.

You may get several nos, but often it only takes a few—or even just one—yes! So don't let fear hold you back. If you won't put yourself out there, you can't win. Give yourself a chance!

Maybe you're thinking, *There just isn't a scholarship out there for me.* Well, think again! Literally billions of dollars are given away each year to help students with college expenses—for all sorts of reasons beyond just academic achievement and sports. Everything from volunteer work to your career goals can qualify you! There are even scholarships given away for being left-handed, creating memes, knitting, being a twin, making the most creative peanut butter sandwich, and having the best zombie apocalypse escape plan! And they're not limited to high school seniors. Whether you're just beginning to think about college, heading off to school, already enrolled, or deciding to go back for a degree, there is money available. All types of students from all sorts of backgrounds have been highly successful in winning scholarships. Somebody is going to get them. It might as well be you!

Scholarship Program Criteria

A scholarship application is the gateway to tens of thousands of dollars. The application form varies from program to program, but most scholarships require students to respond to key components. Committees ask certain questions and seek particular information to determine if you are the right recipient. That's why it pays to think through each part of the application form before you respond: your answers can make a big difference in your results.

The following is a brief overview of the most common components scholarship programs use to evaluate applicants.

ACADEMICS

Most scholarship programs ask students to report their grade point average. In order to qualify, a minimum GPA—varying in increments of .25 on a 4.0 scale (2.75, 3.0, etc.)—is often required. Some programs also have students submit their standardized test scores, transcripts, and/or class rank as well.

Even if your scores or rank are not as high as you'd like, you can still experience success. The truth is, you can have less-than-perfect grades; those imperfect grades just mean you'll have to work harder in other areas to make up the difference. When you're up against students with higher scores, and academics are a factor in the judging, you can't expect to win the money if you're doing no more than they are.

That being said, it's no secret that academic achievement is often highly valued in the scholarship process. In fact, some awards are based solely on this. While there are programs that do not request or judge schoolwork, being prepared in this way opens the door to a much broader range of possibilities.

EXTRACURRICULAR ACTIVITIES

Another key component of the scholarship application is an evaluation of your extracurricular activities—or how you spend your time outside of class. Scholarship committees want to see that you meaningfully participate in your community and are a generally well-rounded person.

Some positive ways to demonstrate your extracurricular involvement are through athletics, volunteer work, organizational membership, and employment. Certain scholarship programs ask specifics such as, "What clubs have you been affiliated with while in high school?" or "Where have you been employed over the past four years?"

To really stand out in this area of the application, I typically recommend that students strive for both "range" and "intensity" in their extracurriculars. I use the word *range* to describe the amount and variety of activities a student participates in. *Intensity*, on the other hand, is how heavily involved and accomplished the applicant is within those activities. Finding a strong balance between range and intensity can demonstrate that you are committed to staying active and involved in the world around you, which is an attractive trait in a scholarship applicant. I discuss this concept more thoroughly in chapter 5 of *Confessions of a Scholarship Winner*.

HONORS AND AWARDS

Being asked to list past honors and awards gives applicants a chance to show the results of their efforts in high school. From winning your conference championship in track to making honor roll to being named employee of the month, you probably have accomplishments that are brag-worthy for scholarship applications.

On the other hand, don't be disheartened if you're lacking a shelf full of honors and awards; there may still be time for you to earn some accolades. Look to participate in competitions and events that you might be particularly good at. Also, think beyond the walls of your school to any other places you may have won an award or been recognized, like at church or in a community organization. Whatever your achievements—big or small—make sure you include them in your application. Personal humility is a wonderful quality, but for your applications, put your best foot forward. This is no time to downplay your accomplishments.

ESSAYS

Applications typically list between one and five essay questions on various topics, including past experiences, hypothetical situations, perspective-based or knowledge-based questions, and sometimes just creative questions like, "If you could have one superpower, what would it be, and why?" By asking students to share in this way, judges gain insight into applicants' characters and personalities. This typically makes essays one of the most influential elements of the scholarship application. Your responses bring life to standardized questions, helping distinguish you from the crowd and giving judges the chance to figure out what makes you a great candidate.

I encourage you to invest the effort and forethought into developing engaging, compelling responses. Use this spot to become more than just another number in the stack of applications! You want the judges to see you as someone they feel they know and connect with. Be willing to open up and share about what makes you *you*. I've devoted chapter 7 of *Confessions of a Scholarship Winner* to showing you how to write the best essay possible.

LETTERS OF RECOMMENDATION

Letters of recommendation confirm to scholarship judges that you are, in fact, just as amazing as your application says! While scholarship committees may want to trust your word about yourself, they often ask that you back up your claims with endorsements from people who know you well. Teachers, coaches, and other credible sources can serve as "star witnesses" and write glowing words that detail why you are the best candidate for a scholarship.

Never underestimate the power these letters can have. Think about a courtroom setting. If a defendant is trying to prove his case and several credible witnesses come forward to verify his story, the jury is much more likely to believe him. Recommenders are witnesses who put their name and reputation on the line to support your "case" about your experiences and potential, as well as your positive traits and character.

Contrary to what you may have heard, finding the recommender with the most prestigious title doesn't necessarily impress scholarship judges if the person doesn't know you. Judges can often see through these generic testimonials. The best recommenders are people who are part of your life and have watched you grow. They can cite specific points in time when you have exhibited admirable qualities, and they can speak firsthand about your qualifications.

For more information on obtaining stellar letters of recommendation, see chapter 8 of *Confessions of a Scholarship Winner*.

VARIABLES

The following items are required less often on scholarship applications; however, when they're requested, it means they're important.

- *Résumés* are formal documents that list your activities and credentials and are required by many competitive programs. Although you fill out most scholarship applications during senior year of high school, judges typically evaluate all four years. The sooner you start thinking about scholarships, the more time you'll have to develop a résumé that will stand out from the competition. I explain how to create one in chapter 8 of my first book, *Confessions of a Scholarship Winner.*

- *Interviews* are necessary for some highly competitive scholarships, particularly for larger programs with the ability to fly in potential scholars from around the country. For example, once I became a finalist for the Coca-Cola scholarship, interviews were used to determine who would ultimately win the national award. In chapter 9 of *Confessions*, I discuss interview techniques and preparation.

- *FAFSA* results, as discussed in chapter 4 of this book, are used by need-based scholarships to determine if a student qualifies for assistance.

- *Auditions or tryouts* are often required by programs associated with performance or the arts.
- *Sample work* may be requested to demonstrate a specific skill or talent. For example, if you are applying for a scholarship that targets aspiring journalists, a writing sample will likely be required.

Need-Based vs. Merit-Based

The biggest distinction between scholarships is need-based versus merit-based. Need-based scholarships factor in a family's financial status to determine if a student is eligible. Some scholarships and grants are given solely on the basis of financial need. For example, many states and schools allocate money for students within a certain financial bracket who meet basic academic criteria.

For those who do not meet the need-based criteria, there is the wonderful world of merit-based scholarships. They are awarded because of a student's accomplishments, ability, involvement, background, unique traits, or potential. *Every* future college student is a candidate for these awards!

Universities, organizations, private donors, and corporate sponsors give merit scholarships for almost anything you can think of—for being the son or daughter of an alum, choosing a certain major, participating in community service, and much more. If you dig deep enough, you'll find ones that match who you are!

How Do You Find Scholarships?

With nearly 2 million different scholarships available, you obviously don't have time to apply for all of them. It's important to narrow down the field and find ones that fit you best. Fortunately, when it comes to this search, you have options!

There are numerous resources available to help you develop a solid list of prospective scholarships that could send you down the road to financial freedom. You may want to jump on the first few you come across; however, I suggest focusing your time on the ones you have the greatest chance of winning. Use the resources outlined here to locate the most fitting scholarships *for you*.

ONLINE SCHOLARSHIP DATABASES

Online databases such as Cappex.com and Unigo.com help narrow your search. After you type in information about yourself, scholarship results are generated that align with your background, interests, and attributes. Most of the databases provide detailed information about scholarship programs and links to their applications.

A downfall of online databases is, they may not match you with every scholarship you're actually eligible to receive. If you don't realize what you're missing, you may miss out on applying for a scholarship that could be perfect for you. Therefore, use more than one database in your efforts (I recommend at least three or four) and compare the results.

There are also some great apps available. If you watch the show *Shark Tank*, you may have heard about Scholly, which is like an online database, but for your smartphone. It can make searching for scholarships super easy, especially when you're on the go.

Conducting your own online search can also be a relatively effective way to find more possibilities. Typing in keywords that match your characteristics, such as "science scholarship," "leadership scholarship," or "returning students scholarship," can often link you to surprisingly well-matched results.

BOOKS

Every year a few authors go to tremendous efforts to bring you massive volumes full of current scholarship listings, with criteria organized and itemized to help you find strong matches. Books such as *The Ultimate Scholarship Book* by Gen and Kelly Tanabe are packed with information that could bring in thousands of dollars for you!

When you reference these publications, you can see all the scholarships available and determine your eligibility for yourself. I strongly recommend using a combination of online resources *and* books.

YOUR HIGH SCHOOL

Most high schools have scholarship resources available to their students. First and foremost among them is your school counselor, who serves as the point person for scholarship programs seeking to reach students at your school. He or she should be able to provide you with the right contacts and information.

Alumni can be a great resource too. Ask your counselor or teachers for names of students who won significant amounts of award money in previous years. Reach out to those winners via e-mail or social media and ask if they'd be willing to share some of their keys to success. More often than not, alumni are excited to let up-and-coming scholarship seekers in on their strategies. They may even agree to help review some of your applications, which would be a major bonus!

Also, be on the lookout for flyers and website updates, and listen for school announcements regarding other prospects.

Remember Small Scholarships

Don't write off scholarships with smaller amounts of award money. Not only do they add to your college fund, but they often have less competition than their larger counterparts. I recently spoke with someone who funded a scholarship and was frustrated that only five people applied. A few of these small awards can really stack up quickly. And when it comes to paying for college, every little bit counts.

COLLEGES AND UNIVERSITIES

Most universities award a variety of their own merit- and need-based scholarships. Once you decide on your top-choice schools, check their websites for their scholarship listings.

Often, universities have separate applications for admissions and merit-based scholarships. Many of the scholarship applications are due around the same time as the college application, and well before you find out if you're admitted, so don't procrastinate. For example, the last day to apply for Vanderbilt's Ingram Scholars Program, which offers students a four-year, full-tuition scholarship (tuition is currently $43,620 per year) plus volunteer service stipends, is December 1—more than a month before the admissions deadline and four months before university acceptance letters are mailed. Be aware of these important dates so you don't miss out on the opportunity for large scholarships offered by your future school!

If you are already enrolled in a college, check its website or financial aid office to see what's open to current attendees.

Civic organizations such as the Rotary Club and the Elks Foundation give back to their communities by helping local students go to college. Even some churches or church denominations offer college scholarships. Survey your community and your region of the country to see who sponsors awards.

Your school counselor will often have this information, but if you are having trouble getting definitive answers, don't hesitate to pick up the phone and ask someone from the organization about available scholarships.

Applying for Scholarships

Once you've built your scholarship résumé and identified the best-fit programs for you, it's time to apply. You've already put in so many hours becoming scholarship-worthy; now put in the effort to make sure you show it! Craft applications that really sell the wonderful person you are. Go beyond the surface, sharing compelling responses that reflect your personality, why you're a strong candidate for each scholarship, and the potential you have for the future.

Your work can result in thousands of dollars in savings! Five hours spent applying for a scholarship that gets you $5,000 for college is like making $1,000 per hour! That's better than any part-time job you'll find! So invest the time and energy necessary to create a standout application.

Learning all you can about each scholarship program will help you develop targeted applications that really highlight what the judges are looking for. Make sure you understand these two things about any scholarship program before you fill out your application:

1. The Why

Each program has its own reasons for giving out award money—whether it's wanting to produce future leaders, motivate volunteers who will go on to impact the world, or support creative types who can make a prom dress from duct tape (yes, there is a scholarship for that!). As much as possible, you need to pinpoint what is motivating the organization's generosity.

2. The Who

Every scholarship group also has its own definition of an ideal candidate. By unearthing a program's reasons for giving away money, you can get a better picture of what a scholarship winner looks like to them. Survey their website, brochure, database descriptions, and any other useful information you can find. Take note of areas the organization stresses and how things are stated:

- What words are used to describe their candidates and values? (For example, you might notice terms such as perseverance, ambition, creativity.)
- Are certain themes repeatedly mentioned (perhaps entrepreneurship or civic duty)?
- Does the organization place a high value on community service? If so, is one certain area of service spoken of more than others?
- What similarities do previous winners of this scholarship share?

From this research, using the hints you've gathered and the qualities the scholarship program seems to value most, you can develop an outline of that organization's ideal candidate. This outline can help you customize your application to specifically appeal to those who are reviewing the applications. Reference it as you're filling out the scholarship application, thinking through how you embody the characteristics the program is looking for.

For example, if you were competing for the Best Buy Scholarship, the outline you write would include the fact that the company values community service and, obviously, technology. When applying for its scholarship, you'd want to highlight your volunteer experience—especially any service related to technological advancement or innovative use. And if the essay topic is "Discuss a moment in your life that made a significant impact," then featuring a situation where you used technology to assist people in need would be a smart approach.

Outlines are quick, simple tools that help you craft responses in a way that lets judges know you took the time to familiarize yourself with their program, you're a great choice for their award, and you really want their scholarship.

Covering the Extras

Scholarships can pay for more than just tuition expenses. Each university has an official cost of attendance that includes housing, food, transportation, books, and personal expenses—all of which scholarships may be used to cover. Students are often surprised to learn that my university cut me a check for about $9,000 per semester for books and living expenses once I moved off campus. When I lived in the dorms and was on the meal plan, I'd still get a few thousand dollars a year because I had enough scholarship money to fund the designated personal expenses in the cost of attendance. Use this as motivation to get as many scholarships as possible. Extra scholarships could eventually mean extra cash in hand.

SWEAT THE DETAILS

When your opportunity to share about yourself is very small, details are HUGE. In most scholarship applications, you have only a few pages to get your point across. Your content may be fantastic and your story engaging, but spelling errors, incorrect punctuation, and awkward wording can easily stand between you and a $50,000 award for college.

There were several times when I thought my application was ready to go . . . and then I realized in my "final" review that I had left a line blank or that a period was missing. With such limited space in the scholarship application and so little that the judges are basing their decisions on, you really want to make sure you don't overlook anything. Careless mistakes can send red flags to scholarship committees, signaling a lack of commitment to the process—or just plain laziness.

As you do your final reviews of your applications, keep in mind the critical areas of spelling, grammar, and punctuation; missing or misunderstood answers; and word limits. This way you won't disqualify yourself.

RECYCLE

Filling out information and writing essays for each scholarship application may seem like a lot of work, but there's a bonus to carefully working through the process on the front end: once you've completed a few, it gets easier! Not only do you achieve a flow and get the hang of how it all works, but you can do a wonderful thing called recycling! Recycling application elements is very similar to traditional recycling. Just like plastic, metal, or paper is passed through a process that makes those materials usable again, you can do the same for your essays, recommendation letters, and more.

Once you've completed one or two applications, you will have a blueprint you can adjust for future applications, whether they're for admissions or scholarships. You don't have to hash out all your activities again—you've already done that! From here on out, you can copy and paste the information into the next application, and modify or improve it as needed.

This makes it easier to submit multiple applications. Just be sure you still take the time to customize each one to the program you're applying for. While recycling is meant to save you hours and effort, don't let it hinder your ability to produce meaningful and focused content.

Another advantage of recycling is that it encourages you to keep refining your application components. As you go along, you'll see bits and pieces that could be worded better for greater impact. This can result in significantly stronger essays and applications that increase your chances of standing out.

Recycling is a secret to simplifying and strengthening your scholarship submissions. You've worked hard to put your first few applications together. Now put them to work for you!

Go for It!

I never want to mislead students into thinking that applying for scholarships is an effortless process. It's not. But if you're motivated to put together standout applications, you can be really successful!

While this chapter has given you a solid overview of scholarships, I go into each area with more detail and guidance in my first book, *Confessions of a Scholarship Winner*. I wrote it as a road map to guide you through your entire scholarship journey. I include information like:

- How to distinguish yourself from other applicants
- Developing range and intensity in extracurricular activities
- Scholar qualities judges are looking for
- Writing winning essays
- "Selling yourself" in applications
- Nailing a scholarship interview
- And much more

I challenge you to find that motivation to win a scholarship, or maybe even several! It's free money, and there's a ton of it available. So go after your share!

SUMMARY POINTS

▶ According to Debt.org, over $46 billion in grants and scholarship dollars is given away each year by the US Department of Education and America's colleges and universities. Beyond that, private sources gift well over another $3 billion.

▶ Scholarship programs commonly use these components to evaluate applicants: academics, extracurricular activities, honors and awards, essays, letters of recommendation, and variable criteria like résumés, interviews, the FAFSA, auditions or tryouts, and sample work.

▶ The best resources for finding scholarships are online scholarship databases, books, your high school, colleges and universities, and your community.

▶ When applying for a scholarship, make sure you get to know the program providing the scholarship by understanding the "why" (the organization's reason and motivation for providing a scholarship) and the "who" (qualities the organization seems to value most in applicants).

▶ As you do your final review of your application, sweat the details like spelling, grammar, and punctuation; missing or misunderstood answers; and word limits.

▶ Once you've completed one or two applications, you will have a blueprint you can recycle and adjust for future applications, making the process progressively easier.

6

PAY AS YOU GO

Working Your Way Through

*The road to success is not easy to navigate,
but with hard work, drive and passion,
it's possible to achieve the American dream.*

Tommy Hilfiger

If you've made it this far in the book, I'm assuming: 1) you really want to graduate college debt-free, and 2) you're willing to do what it takes to make it happen. And often, "what it takes" is work.

The vast majority of college students in the United States today work while attending school. According to a 2015 Georgetown study, a consistent 70 to 80 percent are active in the labor market while getting their education. The Georgetown researchers also found that about two in five undergraduates and three in four graduate students put in at least 30 hours a week on the job. So if you plan to work while attending college, you're in good company!

Although the income you earn may not be enough to fully fund your education, having a job is a great way to fill in the gaps. Even without an abundance of savings or scholarship dollars, plenty of people have still managed to work their way through college and graduate school without student loan debt. So can you!

Considerations

Before we get too deep into strategic discussions about working your way through college, let's first address some considerations that can help you determine the affordability of your education and whether paying as you go is feasible.

The first consideration is the price tag of the school you choose. When you're trying to work your way through, attending an expensive university (the big-ticket ones can run upward of $60,000 per year) isn't as feasible without other significant assistance such as scholarships, financial aid, and/or support from family. Weigh your choice with the financial implications in mind. In chapter 8, we'll discuss how to select a college that's worth it.

Another major consideration is your expenses beyond tuition. It's important to maintain a tight budget and keep your costs down. One area to think through is housing and food. While students typically value the experience of living on campus, it may not be worth it if it causes you to sink into debt that takes years to pay off. The average annual cost of room and board at a public four-year institution is just over $10,000 and about $11,500 at a private four-year school. (And this figure is solely for the academic year—it doesn't cover housing and food during the summer months.) Reducing these costs alone can increase your prospects of graduating debt-free.

If being on campus will break the bank for you, consider less expensive off-campus housing such as splitting an apartment with friends or staying with family, as well as cheaper meal options. We'll dive deeper into budget setting and further ways to save in chapter 9.

Also, it's essential to think through your course load. How much time at a job can you handle while maintaining your schoolwork, and vice versa? If you're being charged by the semester rather than by the credit hour, then take as many credits as you can realistically manage, because they're already paid for. However, enrolling in several classes only helps if you can do well in all of them. Therefore, evaluate your commitments to both work and school, and make sure the combination is something you can sustain. For example, one year you might work 20 hours a week at a part-time job and only take 12 hours of classes per semester, and the next year be able to carry 18 course hours because you secured a paid summer internship and no longer need to work during school.

In any case, remember to consistently re-evaluate how

your schedule and your commitments are meshing. While there may be some long hours and sacrifices along the way, remind yourself: it's only for a season. You're investing in an education that can pay off for the rest of your life. Doing it debt-free is a cause well worth the fight!

Tuition Payment Plans

If you know you can afford to pay for college as you go, but may not be able to cover the total cost upfront each semester, consider signing up for tuition payment plans. This will allow you to spread the costs into more manageable installments. Keep in mind, a small fee may be added. Explore what your school offers and if there is a great choice that suits your needs.

Job Opportunities

There's not a "one size fits all" approach to working your way through college. Who you work for, when you work, and how you work—your possibilities are virtually endless! And you don't have to pick just one. You could sign up for work-study and then freelance on the side. Or you could take a part-time position on weekends and then intern during the summer.

As we explore the primary categories of job opportunities for college students, think through which ones might be best for you.

WORK-STUDY

As we discussed in chapter 4, students demonstrating financial need are often offered a work-study option as part of their financial aid package. Work-study is a federal program that helps students earn money through part-time work at the school; at a federal, state, or local public agency; at a private non-profit; or at a for-profit organization. Students work during the school year, earning up to the fixed amount of money stated in their financial aid award letter, and are guaranteed to receive at least the current federal minimum wage.

Just because you are eligible for work-study, however, doesn't mean you're guaranteed a particular job. You will still need to find the right position and apply for it, just like any other job. Get in touch with your campus employment office to learn more about what's available.

A key benefit of work-study is that the money doesn't count against you on the FAFSA in following years. Which means that if you're relying on financial aid in subsequent years, these earnings won't decrease your eligibility like other income can. If you have the opportunity to participate in work-study, weigh it against other options. Also, don't just take the first position you find. Do your homework so you can find the right spot for you.

....

INTERNSHIPS

....

An internship is a temporary position offered by a company or organization that gives a student real-world experience, knowledge, and skills relevant to a particular career field. Many of these opportunities don't pay, and that's okay because, in a sense, they tend to pay off down the road. Still, there are some really great ones that do offer students a stipend or wage. You shouldn't make your decision based solely on money, but if you'll be working anyway, getting paid while completing an internship is a pretty great way to go.

Interning while in college provides a host of benefits that can catapult you into your post-college career. So if you're going to take one of these positions, which I highly recommend, leverage it for future success by being strategic about how and where you work. You want to stretch the value beyond a bullet point on your résumé and maximize the time invested.

A few ways to get the most out of your internship include:

Earning Credit

Nearly all colleges and universities grant students the opportunity to earn credit for their internship efforts. It's a nice way to get a leg up on the competition after you graduate, even as you complete your studies. When enrolling for internship credit with your school, do make sure the additional credits will apply toward your graduation curriculum.

Gaining Experience

Internships give students a "behind the curtain" look at a career they're interested in. This insider's view can further confirm one's career path or encourage a shift in direction—either of which can help establish you in your future line of work that much sooner.

For example, if you dream of being on the business side of the fashion industry, a summer internship with a New York designer may verify this is the type of job for you and that you're headed in the right direction, or lead you to realize it's not as glamorous as you imagined and point you toward a business position in another field. Either way, you'll know before graduation and have time to plan. And since a segment of employers require some degree of experience before they will hire you, internships can help fulfill those requirements.

Making Connections

Many students walk away from internships with major connections that pay off. A lot of doors opened for me as a result of mentors and supervisors I got to know through internships. This made the experience even more valuable in the long run.

To optimize your networking potential:

- *Build a good working relationship with your supervisor.* This person not only has influence within the company or organization but could also serve as an excellent recommendation in the future.
- *Be a team player.* Not all internships are glamorous, and many times you'll end up doing grunt work. Stay positive, work hard, and be ready to pitch in whenever the opportunity presents itself. You never know who's watching and what kind of impact your good attitude could have.
- *Prepare to network.* Interns are often invited to events and professional meetings that students wouldn't have access to otherwise. Carry a business card, be engaged and respectful, and be diligent about follow-up. If someone gives you their business card, send them a quick thank-you e-mail so that you stay on their radar. It's a great way to start expanding your network.

Intentional Internship

A friend of mine who knew she wanted to be a writer chose to attend a small college in the Chicago suburbs. A main reason for her decision was the school's proximity to numerous publishers.

Over her four years there, she secured campus jobs in her field of interest, including serving as yearbook editor and a work-study position that let her write for the school's alumni magazine. During her junior year, a professor helped arrange a summer internship at her favorite magazine. Not only did she earn credit toward her degree, but when the experience was over, she was sure she wanted a career in publishing specifically. Just as she was graduating, the magazine contacted her about an open editorial position—and weeks later, she was hired! That position helped spark a career that has included writing books and editing numerous *New York Times* bestsellers.

Her inspiring story goes to show that being intentional with your college internships and other job opportunities can boost your career in a major way!

CO-OPS

Cooperative education programs, or co-ops, are partnerships between schools and employers that allow students to receive paid career training within their field of study. Co-ops make it possible for participants to work alongside professionals on real-world projects, make an income, and in some cases, earn credit.

Occasionally the terms *co-op* and *internship* are used interchangeably; however, a primary difference is that co-op students usually stop taking classes to work full-time, whereas an internship can be done part-time while still maintaining a normal class schedule. The most common co-op model alternates between a semester of classes and a semester of full-time work. Also, co-op students usually fill an actual role within the corporate structure, whereas internships are often add-on positions in a company. Consequently, your earning potential with a co-op is generally much higher.

A major benefit of co-ops is that what you earn doesn't count against you on the FAFSA and is excluded in the calculation of your EFC. However, it may still affect state and school-based aid. Be sure to speak with your financial aid officer to verify how this option could affect your package.

In the world beyond campus, companies will often only consider applicants with at least a year's worth of experience in the field—and sometimes they want even more than that—which can be a significant challenge for new graduates. Co-ops are a great way to build that experience. Because co-op students have worked full-time for several months, they generally graduate with more established professional relationships and project experience than their peers.

It's important to note: not all universities or majors offer co-ops. If yours does, check to see what rules and financial implications apply. You may not have to pay standard tuition while completing a co-op, but some sort of smaller fee is possible. Do your research to explore if a co-op program is right for you.

TRADITIONAL JOBS

There are thousands of jobs beyond those tied to your financial aid package or school programs. Full- or part-time work is available pretty much anywhere! From waiting restaurant tables to working at a nursing home to retail positions at the mall, these jobs all have the potential to help you pay for your college education. And because they aren't regulated by your school, your income and hours aren't restricted. Plus, you are still earning experience that can help you in the job hunt after you graduate.

Take your time to find a job that is flexible (or that fits within your class schedule), pays well, and benefits your résumé in the future.

FREELANCING

Building business as a freelancer is a great way for college students to make money while also maintaining a high level of flexibility. If you have a skill that will bring value to others, outsourcing platforms and smartphone apps have made it easier than ever to offer and get paid for your services.

Maybe you've got a knack for designing logos or websites . . . or perhaps you'd make a great personal assistant or proofreader. With the growth of websites like Upwork, TaskRabbit, and Freelancer, you can be up and running in a matter of minutes. Also, companies like Uber, Lyft, and Handy provide other flexible options for work. And that's just scratching the surface!

EMPLOYMENT AT A COLLEGE

During a graduate school class, the instructor had us go around the room and introduce ourselves. I was surprised to learn that over half of my peers in that course worked for the university! I later learned they were receiving an 80 percent discount on tuition in addition to their wages.

Many colleges and universities offer extensive discounts to their employees. Staff positions aren't just limited to teaching; a multitude of jobs are needed to keep a campus running smoothly. While this may not be the most traditional route to a degree, the savings can be huge! Think about it: If you already plan on getting a degree and you were going to work somewhere anyway, then a salaried, staff position at your school is like getting a big bonus! As a result of your job, you not only receive a paycheck but a vastly reduced school bill.

This works especially well for graduate students, who typically already have a bachelor's degree under their belt and are better qualified for university-based positions. The tuition break often extends to dependent students as well; therefore, parents employed at universities can be a source of major discounts!

Assistantships are also strong options for college-affiliated employment. They are designed to provide paid, part-time, academic-related work to graduate students. The benefits can vary between universities and programs, though they often include hourly pay, tuition discounts, or a combination of both.

TUITION ASSISTANCE PROGRAMS

Tuition assistance programs are employer-sponsored benefit programs that reimburse employees for education expenses. They can be particularly helpful for students who delayed starting college, have a family to support, or decide to pursue graduate school after entering the workplace. Being able to maintain a career and earn a living while receiving a significant discount toward a degree is a great option!

These programs are typically managed through a company's human resources department. Internal Revenue Service regulations allow employers to provide up to $5,250 to employees each year tax-free, leading many employers to stay within that limit. Still, these programs can vary significantly depending on the company. Here are some of those ways:

- *GPA requirements.* Employees may need to maintain a minimum GPA to remain eligible for assistance.
- *Timing.* Some programs will pay upfront for tuition while others reimburse the employee for tuition upon receipt of grades.
- *Post-degree commitment.* Companies may require employees to continue working for them for a certain period of time after graduation.
- *Limitations.* The program may only be offered to specified employees, or the areas of study may be restricted. For example, an employer might only pay toward tuition for middle management or above, or if the coursework directly relates to an individual's job description.
- *Logistics.* The process to secure funding with some companies may be more complicated than with others: employees may have to go through an interview or multilevel approval process first.
- *Completion schedule.* The length of time a company will continue paying toward an employee's degree may be limited.

Future Income Commitments (The Pay It Forward Movement)

There is a new possibility on the college-finance horizon. It is based on the idea of students committing a certain portion of their future income to pay for their current college costs. With this alternative, students wouldn't have to make school payments upfront; instead, they would sign a contract agreeing to pay back a certain percentage to the state upon entering the workforce. The proposed model would require them to commit 1 percent of their annual income for each year of college completed for 25 years after graduation. Therefore, with a four-year education, you'd agree to give 4 percent of your income annually. The vision is that as students graduate and start paying back their percentages, they're essentially paying for the next class of students to get degrees.

Currently, several states are considering legislation around this idea and exploring pilot programs. A few startups have tried a similar model, but this is very much an innovation in progress. Though its future is unclear, it is definitely an option worth keeping an eye on in the coming years.

Finding Jobs

Now that you have a better idea of the types of jobs available to working college students, how do you go about locating the position for you? Try these ideas.

DISCOVER YOUR SCHOOL'S
AVAILABLE RESOURCES

Colleges and universities have a vested interest in providing students with powerful resources to help in their job search: they know that successful grads will attract future applicants. Thus, most schools have a career center where students can go for advice, assessment testing, job listings, employer-information sessions, career-fair information, résumé and cover letter review, recruiting, and career libraries. Yours may also have great online portals. Unfortunately, it's not un-common for students to go their entire college experience without taking advantage of these free resources. Educate yourself about what your school offers, and maximize those resources to land your dream job, both while you're in college and once you graduate.

TAKE ADVANTAGE OF CAREER CENTER EVENTS

Your college's career center is the hub for potential employ-ers coming to campus. When it sponsors job and internship fairs at your school, make sure you sign up and show up. Being able to meet with employers face-to-face greatly in-creases your chances of getting hired. Plus, these meet-and-greets are good practice for networking events and lengthier job interviews that will inevitably be part of your future.

Next-Level Jobs

In our rapidly changing world, each year brings more and more opportunities for students to earn a career-advancing certification or an associate's degree prior to finishing a four-year degree. No longer do high schools just offer shop class, for example. Today it's possible to get trade-school certification along with your diploma! And I've already shared in chapter 3 about opportunities for pre-college credit.

Now let's take this strategy a step further. If you've completed specialized training early on, this can open wide the door for you to work smarter, not harder in college—securing higher-paying positions because of your greater experience.

Let's say you're studying medicine. If you have received EMT training, why not choose that kind of work versus a fast-food job while you earn your degree? The experience can be invaluable to your career—and to your bank account, as you'll quickly notice the difference that even $5 more per hour makes.

NETWORK

Be bold enough to try developing great professional relationships beyond your campus community. You'd be surprised at how many working adults are glad to share their experiences with college students. Use LinkedIn and résumé networking groups to meet people who could not only give you invaluable advice but also potentially open career doors. Invite someone to coffee and ask if you can pick his or her brain. Even if that person doesn't have a job recommendation the first time you meet, he or she will likely have some useful insights and could be a great resource in the future.

APPLY FOR AN ON-CAMPUS JOB

Even if you don't qualify for work-study, you may still be able to snag a job on campus. See if your school's career center has a customized job website; many schools do, and they're helpful with both on- and off-campus openings. Also, talk to a career center advisor about prospective campus jobs. These positions may not pay as much as some off-campus jobs, but the convenience factor is big—you save commute time and have additional opportunities to build your community of on-campus friends. And because you're working at your school, you may be permitted to do homework if there is a lull during hours.

USE ONLINE RESOURCES

There are numerous websites, apps, and resources to help students locate great jobs. Wayup.com and Collegerecruiter .com specifically cater to college students, while standard career websites like Monster.com and LinkedIn can also yield great opportunities. Pursue freelance options through sites like Fiverr.com and Elance.com.

....

All this should encourage you that the college job of your dreams is within your reach. That's why it's worth a bit of extra energy in the search process: because there's nothing like finding work that will truly make you happy *and* help you build career skills. Making money is, of course, important to your debt-free goals, but it's a lot more fun when you can achieve your financial goals through fulfilling work. Be willing to do what it takes, give it your best effort, and keep your eyes on the prize: the freedom of a debt-free future is priceless.

Tuition-Free Schools

Did you know there are schools that have built their tuition model with working students in mind? That's right! They offer free tuition in exchange for a work or service commitment. For example, students at College of the Ozarks in Missouri work 10 to 15 hours per week and two 40-hour weeks during the summer in exchange for full tuition. The school also has a summer program available to help with room and board. Colleges like Berea in Kentucky and Deep Springs in California follow similar models.

Some tuition-free schools, on the other hand, require a

future work commitment or term of service rather than expecting students to work while in college. The most widely known examples of this are the US Coast Guard Academy in Connecticut, the US Naval Academy in Maryland, the US Military Academy in New York, the US Air Force Academy in Colorado, and the US Merchant Marine Academy in New York. All of these schools have strict admission requirements and expect graduates to serve at least five years of active duty upon completion of their education. Another version of this is the CUNY (City University of New York) Teacher Academy, which provides four-year tuition scholarships for qualified students pursuing a math or science degree. In exchange, students commit to teaching in New York City public schools for two years after graduation.

There are also schools that waive tuition costs based on a student's exemplary achievements, such as Macaulay Honors College at CUNY, Webb Institute in New York, and the Curtis Institute of Music in Philadelphia. These schools challenge students to excel in their chosen field. For example, at the Webb Institute, each student earns a dual degree in naval architecture and marine engineering.

Finally, one major proposal in recent years—called America's College Promise—would make two years of community college free so that people could earn half of their bachelor's degree and gain some career skills at no cost.

Programs like Tennessee Promise have laid the groundwork for the possibilities nationwide, and though at the time of this writing the program has not yet been signed into law, there is a good chance that free community colleges will become a national norm in coming years.

The Challenges

Both researchers and financial experts recommend working through college because of the career and monetary benefits. However, holding a job while going to school can also present some challenges.

The first is finding a balance between work, life, and school. Studies have shown that too many hours on the job while attending college increases the likelihood that you will take more than four years to graduate. An even worse scenario would be to get too burnt out to graduate at all, especially if you have accumulated any debt. If you're struggling to keep up with your coursework because you're exhausted or your attention is so divided, then it's counterproductive and you need to re-evaluate.

The sweet spot for full-time students during the school year seems to be between 10 and 20 work hours per week. This amount of time lets you earn enough money to help cover costs and gain notable job experience, while also striking a balance that encourages academic success. Also, remember to maximize summers and holiday breaks. Capitalize on those times when school isn't in session to work more hours and save up for when classes start back up again.

Another challenge is the potential impact this income may have on your financial aid package. As we saw in chapter 4, the FAFSA factors both parent and student income into the Expected Family Contribution (EFC) equation. Fortunately, the FAFSA does allow students to earn up to a certain amount before it increases their EFC.

For the 2016–17 school year, dependent students are allowed up to $6,400 in earnings without affecting their aid package. Independent student allowances start at $9,960 and range upward based on marital status and number of children. Fifty percent of earnings above that threshold are expected to go toward college expenses, therefore increasing a student's EFC by 50 cents for every dollar. A good thing about work-study is that it is exempt, meaning that it doesn't count as income; it is calculated as financial aid. Therefore, it doesn't go against your earnings limits or impact your aid formula the following year.

Also, we said in chapter 4 that student assets, which include money sitting in a student's bank account, are figured in at a rate of 20 percent—far more than the rate for parental assets. This means that every $1,000 sitting in a student's savings account increases his or her EFC by $200. So be mindful of your savings and how those dollars could impact your financial aid eligibility.

I've said it already, but it bears repeating: working beyond a certain point could mean sacrificing some significant need-based aid. It may be worth it in your situation; however, before diving headfirst into high earnings while in college, make sure you fully understand the implications the money could have on your financial aid status as you evaluate what's best for you.

Consider It a Plus

Whether you *want* to work while in college, or whether it's a necessity, consider it a plus. Studies show that students who work a modest 10 to 15 hours per week are more likely to succeed in college than those who don't work at all. And as we've discussed, having a job while earning a degree doesn't hurt your career prospects either! Those additional years of work experience and service are a prime way to build up your résumé in ways that will appeal to employers.

For sure, balancing work and school has its challenges. You'll sometimes feel as if you're performing a juggling act, especially during crunch times like finals week. But it can also foster qualities that are known to produce success, such as a greater sense of responsibility, a better ability to organize yourself, and a stronger work ethic. So be strategic in your pursuit and embrace the opportunities in front of you. Giving up some time to work during college can pay enormous dividends, especially considering the money and stress you'll save by not having debt when you graduate. The work you do will not go to waste!

SUMMARY POINTS

▶ When developing your strategy for working your way through college, it's important to consider factors such as the price tag of the school you choose to attend, your expenses beyond tuition, and your course load.

▶ The range of job opportunities taken on by college students primarily falls under these categories: work-study, internships, co-ops, traditional jobs, freelancing, and being employed by a college.

▶ There are many ways to locate college jobs. Among them are school resources, career center events, networking, on-campus job boards, and online tools.

▶ Tuition-free schools are a viable option, offering a free education in exchange for a work or service commitment.

▶ Remember to find the right work, life, and school balance, as well as evaluate how earnings from work might impact your financial aid package.

7

NAVIGATING DEBT

A Dangerous Road

College is part of the American Dream.
It shouldn't be part of a financial nightmare for families.

Barbara Mikuski

I recently had a conversation with a friend who was about to graduate from one of the most prestigious law schools in the country. I expected her to be elated when I asked about life after graduation, but instead, my questions seemed to stir up some ominous feelings. "Actually . . . ," she confessed, "I'm pretty terrified. I'm not sure my new job is going to be enough."

She went on to explain, "I was clueless about the magnitude of what I was signing on for when I started taking out student loans seven years ago." She was 18 at the time and didn't even have her own bank account yet. Now she is $220,000 in debt and face to face with the serious realities of student loan burden. Her payment each month will be more than most people's mortgage. Essentially, she will be paying for a house she doesn't get to live in. She told me, "Kristina, I wish I had really understood what I was getting into."

Unfortunately, her story isn't all that rare. I've heard from countless others who are feeling the burden of student loans. In fact, it's their stories that have been some of my biggest motivators for writing *this* book. I have a passion to help students find other ways to pay for college and avoid the weight of debt.

Alarming Truths about Student Debt

You've probably seen plenty of articles and news clips regarding student loans. It seems like every week, another story comes out about navigating the challenges. Do you know why? Because they're a *major* issue for college students today! Here are some startling statistics:

- US students are $1.2 trillion in college debt, with $3,000 more being accrued per second. (Debt.org)
- Student loans are up by nearly 85 percent since the latest recession ended in 2014, and are "the only type of consumer debt not decreasing." (Experian Study)
- The average college graduate in 2014 owed $33,000 in student loans. (Debt.org)
- Graduate students are racking up even greater debt than undergraduates: 35 percent borrow between

$100,00 and $150,000 by the time they earn that additional degree. (Jason Delisle, director of New America's Federal Education Budget Project)

- For the class of 2015 there's a rising unemployment rate of 7.2 percent and an underemployment rate of 14.9 percent, meaning that colleges can guarantee you a degree, but they can't guarantee you a great job in exchange for your investment. (The Economic Policy Institute)
- Data released in the fall of 2015 by the Obama Administration indicated that "more than one out of every three student loan borrowers nationwide failed to make any progress repaying his or her loans within three years."

As you can see, the numbers are pretty scary. A five-minute Internet search can yield thousands of articles and posts about people lamenting their decision to borrow excessive amounts to pay for a degree that wasn't really worth what they're paying now. While student loans may be very commonplace among your peers, and colleges may declare them "no big deal," they should definitely not be taken lightly. They are debt, after all, and as we discussed in chapter 1, debt should be strongly avoided. Therefore, I write this chapter with reluctance.

My greatest goal with this book is to help you figure out

how to pay for college without one dollar of debt. My hope is that you will use the other strategies in this book and never need to refer to this chapter again. However, I understand some of you will still end up traveling this dangerous road and choose to borrow a small amount rather than fall short on a college degree. I would rather take the time to write on this subject than leave you without any guidance. So . . . keeping in mind that a student loan should be your *very last resort*, let's go over what you need to know. The more careful you are now, the better off you'll be. I promise you, your future self will thank you for not taking on more debt than was absolutely necessary.

Student Loans 101

Student loans can be obtained from a multitude of places including federal and state governments, schools, banks, and credit unions. Before you make a borrowing decision, you'll want to understand the distinctions between these sources to help you determine which loan will come at the least cost to you.

FEDERAL VS. PRIVATE

While the choices are numerous, the entities that offer student loans fall into two main categories: federal or private. Federal student loans are funded by the US government, whereas private student loans are provided by lenders such as banks, credit unions, state agencies, and schools. Here are some key differences:

FEDERAL LOANS	PRIVATE LOANS
Offer fixed interest rates for the life of the loan.	May have variable interest rates and are typically more costly than federal loans, with some rates reaching over 18 percent, resulting in a much higher repayment amount.
May offer income-based repayment, meaning the monthly payment is calculated as a percentage of your income.	Typically do not offer an income-based repayment option.
Repayment isn't required until a student is either no longer in school or has switched to less than half-time enrollment.	Many require students to begin repayment while they're still in school.
Most don't require a credit check or co-signer.	Credit checks or co-signing more commonly required.
Can be combined into a single, *direct consolidation loan*, which offers advantages like flexible repayment options, one lender/ one monthly payment, and reduced payments.	Cannot be used with a *direct consolidation loan* program.

FEDERAL LOANS	PRIVATE LOANS
May be eligible for *public service* or *teacher loan forgiveness* to reduce or eliminate the balance of a student's loans after a certain number of qualifying payments have been made while he or she works for a qualified employer.	Private loans almost never offer loan-forgiveness programs.

SUBSIDIZED VS. UNSUBSIDIZED

Federal student loans come in two forms: subsidized and unsubsidized. Subsidized loans are need-based loans that offer an extra benefit to the borrower, such as deferred interest payments. This means that while you are in school, the government or another group pays the interest. Unsubsidized loans, on the other hand, are available to students and families regardless of financial need. With these loans, however, interest often begins accumulating the moment a student signs the paperwork.

There are two subsidized options for students who show exceptional need: the Direct Subsidized Loan, which is available to qualifying undergrads at any college, and the Federal Perkins Loan, offered to college and graduate students at participating schools. The Perkins Loan is funded by the federal government but managed by each individual school enrolled in the program.

There are also two types of unsubsidized loans: the Direct Unsubsidized Loan, which is open to any student regardless of financial need, and the Direct Plus Loan, which is available to graduate students or parents of dependent undergrads as long as they have good credit. The amount of either loan is calculated by the school's cost of attendance minus any other aid received.

WHERE TO START

The best student loans available to you typically come in your financial aid package. Borrow federal loans first; they're the place to start because they usually offer the lowest interest rates and most reasonable repayment options. If you're offered subsidized loans, use those before considering unsubsidized loans.

Next, look at state-administered or state-sponsored loans. The qualifications are similar to federal loans, and some of the advantages—like low interest and fixed rates—may still apply, although their rates are usually a bit higher than federal ones. Sites like CollegeScholarships.org and GoCollege.com have an A-Z list of what's available by state.

Finally, your absolute last resort should be private student loans. As discussed, these are typically the most expensive kind, and they come with the fewest potential benefits and protections. Their variable interest rates can also be very confusing and hard to keep track of. Lenders will often advertise an incredibly low rate, but be wary: few families qualify for the best rates. These lenders also frequently tout their easy application process, which can distract families from better loans that might be available.

To restate, here's the order of preference for loans:

1. Federal subsidized loans
2. Federal unsubsidized loans
3. State-sponsored loans
4. Private loans

If you decide to pursue private loans, evaluate multiple options. The problem with exploring only one is that these companies rarely disclose their pricing up front, making it difficult to anticipate the real rates and terms you will have to live with. By considering multiple loans, you can choose the offer with the best numbers. Even a small rate change can equal thousands of dollars in savings over the life of a loan.

Top Five Tips for Borrowing Wisely

No one really *enjoys* thinking about student loans, but I encourage you to look at them from all angles. Taking them on will be a years-long commitment, so arm yourself with all the information you can get. These five tips will help you cover your bases.

1. UNDERSTAND WHAT YOU'RE SIGNING

Make sure you're clear on a loan's terms and conditions. You want to know the exact implications of borrowing this money, including:

- *Rates.* What is your interest rate, and is your interest rate fixed or variable, meaning: will it always stay the same, or will it fluctuate with the markets?
- *Fees.* Are there any fees? Most loans, including federal loans, have some. They are a portion of your total loan amount, typically ranging from 1 to 5 percent. The money is often deducted from your student loan total before you receive the money. Still, you are responsible for repaying the full loan amount.
- *The total cost of this loan.* How much will you actually be paying back over the life of the loan? With interest and fees factored in, it's typically far more than the original amount you borrowed.
- *Your grace period.* How long do you have after graduation before you are required to start paying

back the loan? The standard time frame is six months, though some loans offer no grace period.

- *Projected monthly payments.* What will you be required to pay each month? You can visit StudentLoans.gov and use their repayment calculator to get a better idea of what your monthly amount will be after graduation. There are also calculators available on other websites like Bankrate.com and SallieMae.com.

2. CONSIDER ALTERNATIVES

It may feel like student loans are your only option, especially when you're really sold on a particular school. But before signing on the dotted line, make sure you've assessed every alternative. If the debt you're about to agree to seems insurmountable, perhaps you should consider a more affordable college, or starting at a community college and then later transferring to a four-year school. Or maybe you can get a part-time job, continue applying for scholarships throughout college, or implement cost-cutting budget measures.

3. ASK QUESTIONS

If the terms seem a bit murky or you're not clear on the exact interest rates you'll be paying after graduation, have your financial aid officer or loan administrator clarify things. Don't be afraid to ask questions if you're unsure of anything related to this process. Taking out a loan is a big decision, and you have the right to be completely informed about what you're getting into.

4. KEEP GREAT RECORDS

College students tend to move around a lot. You may spend one school year living on campus, be someplace else for the summer, and then choose a spot off campus the next school year. You may even end up transferring schools at some point. That said, it's important to keep good records of any and all student loans. Create a spreadsheet with lender names, contact information, balances, and the repayment status for each of your loans. Then, whenever you change your address, e-mail, or phone number, contact each lender to update your information.

If you're not sure who the lender is on your federal student loan, visit the National Student Loan Database System website, where you can log in and get key information pertaining to your loans.

5. WISELY PLAN YOUR COURSE LOAD

If you're going to college on borrowed money, you have even more incentive to graduate in four years. Each additional year could create a need for more loans, on top of the accumulating interest you may have on outstanding balances. So be diligent about planning your course load, and only take classes that count toward your graduation requirements. Even if you're uncertain about what you want to major in freshman year, make sure the classes you're taking fulfill your general education or elective requirements. Don't let a lack of planning lead to thousands of dollars in additional debt.

A Parent's or Mentor's Role

The ins and outs of student loans are a lot to process. Most young adults have very little experience managing their own money or sorting through legally binding documents. Therefore, when an overwhelming amount of financial information is thrown at them upon entering college, they may be prone to just start signing on the dotted line.

Parents and mentors can play a significant role in helping students work through the information: explaining loan terms and conditions, analyzing the options, and setting up account management plans so their student stays organized. Taking on a loan is a huge decision for a young person, one he or she admittedly may not fully understand or be confident about. Your help in breaking things down and working through the details can significantly impact how well the student you care about navigates this process.

A word of caution: be extremely careful about agreeing to co-sign for a student loan.

With their limited or non-existent credit history, students can find it difficult to get approved for the best private loan rates, or to even be approved at all. In their desire to help, it's all too common for parents, family members, or mentors to quickly agree to co-sign for student debt, not realizing the significance of this commitment. "There's no boxed warning label that says co-signing a student loan may be hazardous to your wealth," says college debt expert Mark Kantrowitz. "On this loan, you're giving them the keys to your car . . . the ability to ruin your credit."

If the student fails to pay back the loan on which you co-signed, you are responsible for repayment. And should the student default on the loan, your credit will be damaged too. It's also important to note that student loan debt doesn't go away until it is paid off. Even if bankruptcy is declared, you still owe this money.

Therefore, think long and hard before signing on. It may feel harsh to say no, but in the long run, that's much simpler than carrying the burden of loans on someone else's behalf. And while a student's dreams of college are important, so are your retirement goals and the ability to pay your own bills. Using the many other strategies in this book, you can still be highly involved in helping your student pursue an education without assuming the implications of his or her debt.

Temptations to Avoid

If you end up taking out student loans, it doesn't automatically mean you'll be exclusively eating mac 'n' cheese for the next 10 years, or that you won't be able to purchase a home until you're 80 . . . However, you do need to be proactive and disciplined. Avoid the common temptations that can lead to greater financial burdens than necessary, such as:

BORROWING
MORE THAN YOU NEED

You may know of students who have taken out private student loans but funded things far beyond just educational expenses with that money. It's a very easy trap to fall into. Since private lenders require little accountability about how their money gets spent, some students use the payout for things like spending money, summer living expenses, trips, and gadgets. After all the warnings you've read in this section, that may sound outrageous, but it happens far more often than you think. What seems like "easy money" up front is by no means easy if in the long run you end up paying far more than the original amount.

BEING UNREALISTIC ABOUT
YOUR ABILITY TO REPAY

Think through what repaying student loans will look like after graduation, and don't overestimate your potential income. Will you truly be able to afford the monthly payment? Exorbitant student loan obligations can really restrict you, sometimes forcing you to take a job just for a higher salary versus one that's truly a great career move. And even that higher-paying job may not be enough. Don't put yourself in a position where you severely limit your freedom in the future.

PROLONGING THE START OF PAYMENTS

Unless you have a subsidized student loan or a special offer (like a 0 percent APR [annual percentage rate] for one year), your interest will start accruing the day you sign the papers. Meaning, even if you are given permission to skip payments while in school (and for a "grace period" after graduation), your loan doesn't stop growing. And though it's defined in the terms, many students are surprised to realize their $15,000 private loan from freshman year has ballooned to over $20,000 upon graduation. While sometimes you're unable to start paying the loans immediately, try making at least a basic interest payment to avoid compounding debt.

FALLING VICTIM TO PREDATORY
STUDENT LOAN SCAMS

Not all "lenders" are legit. Sometimes shady companies will market themselves with official-looking names and logos in an attempt to draw in borrowers. Many will offer free bonuses or other rewards in exchange for your business. So thoroughly research any lender you are considering. Check with your school to see if the company is on their recommended lenders list, and if not, follow up with your state attorney general's office about whether the company is officially registered and whether complaints have been filed against it. Also, be slow to dole out your social security number and other personal information. About 7 percent of people 16 and older were victims of identity theft in 2014, reports the Bureau of Justice's *Victims of Identity Theft* bulletin. Sadly, there are individuals and companies out there who prey on students who are simply trying to afford an education. Educate yourself so you don't become a victim.

Be Leery of Credit Cards

I've saved this section for the end, as it shouldn't even be a reasonable option for college debt. Since 2009 and the passing of the Credit CARD (Card Accountability Responsibility and Disclosure) Act, it has become increasingly difficult for students to be approved for a credit card without a co-signing adult. These restrictions have been a welcomed change among financial experts, as credit cards represent the most expensive money students can borrow. The sponsoring companies may draw you in with low interest rates initially, but then increase those rates significantly down the road. Or they may entice you with perks such as free miles, a couple of hundred dollars as a "signing bonus," or no annual fee for the first year. In most cases, the benefits don't come close to the eventual costs. And while these cards are one way to establish credit, the problem comes when you don't pay them off every month. Money is already tight enough during the college years. Don't let the appeal of quick, easy money cloud the reality of 20 percent (or higher!) interest rates. They can be crippling, especially if you won't be able to really start paying down your balances until after graduation.

Be wise and very leery of the dangers of credit card debt. Credit cards are NOT the way to pay for college!

My Hope for You

I'll never encourage you to take on student loans. With all the other alternatives for college funding that are out there—and so many of them discussed in this book—school loans should be your last choice.

You may not want to think through the long-term effects of decisions like this right now, but trust me . . . it's better than living with the consequences after college. Do your future self a favor and proceed through student loan territory with extreme caution. My hope for you is to start your career as debt-free and stress-free as possible!

SUMMARY POINTS

▶ Student loans are an enormous challenge for many students. According to Debt.org, US students are $1.2 trillion in college debt, and the numbers are increasing by the second.

▶ The biggest distinctions to understand when evaluating student loans are federal versus private, and subsidized versus unsubsidized.

▶ The order of preference for student loans is federal subsidized loans first, then federal unsubsidized loans, followed by state-sponsored loans, and finally, as a last resort, private loans.

▶ To borrow wisely, make sure you: understand what you're signing, consider alternatives, ask questions, keep great records, and wisely plan your course load.

▶ Avoid these common temptations surrounding student loans: borrowing more than you need, being unrealistic about your ability to repay, prolonging the start of payments, and falling victim to predatory student loan scams.

8

MAKE COLLEGE WORTH IT

Schools & Majors That Pay Off

*My philosophy is that not only are you responsible
for your life, but doing the best at this moment
puts you in the best place for the next moment.*

Oprah Winfrey

Because getting a degree is one of the biggest investments you'll make in your life, you should treat it as
just that: an investment. Not only is your money involved,
but so are your time and energy. With thousands of colleges
and majors to pick from, obviously not all things are equal
and not every one is right for you. Today more than ever, it's
important to explore beneath the surface and make a choice
that will pay off in the long run.

If you were buying a new house, you'd want to evaluate every detail of that investment. When I purchased my
first home, I took a tour of it, learned about the builder and

quality of the home, acquainted myself with the neighborhood, researched area crime rates and the price of comparable properties, and had it inspected for any issues or defects—all to ultimately determine if it would meet my needs and be worth the price.

Just as much or more energy should be put into evaluating the investment of a college degree.

According to the College Board, higher-education costs rose 10 percent between 2010 and 2015. The average price of a four-year degree at a public school is just over $78,000 and is nearly $176,000 at a private school. Unfortunately, in spite of these massive costs, you're not guaranteed a job after graduation, or even an open door to your career of choice.

Some colleges, however, do statistically offer a better chance of capturing that ideal job after graduation. And many schools are striving to make sure students get the best return on their investment. Therefore, it's important to make honest assessments and choose a school that will not only provide a quality education but can kick-start your career. This front-end effort can lead to much higher earnings and invaluable job satisfaction in the long run.

College Rankings

When considering which college is the best to attend, a lot of students immediately check where the schools rank nationally and regionally according to the lists published each year by various organizations—the most popular being *US News & World Report*. It's very tempting to view these recommendations as live-or-die statistics and consequently overemphasize a school's place on a list (or absence from it) in your decision making. Yet there's a lot more to a school than this. A tremendous number of colleges and universities don't make the Top 20, but that doesn't mean they're not excellent in their own right. And one of them could be absolutely perfect for you.

Here are other important questions to consider as you begin evaluating colleges:

- What is the student-to-faculty ratio and class size?
- What is the culture of the school and its surrounding area?
- What about its location? Do I prefer living in or near a large city, or do I like a more small-town or rural setting? Where do most of the students come from?
- Will I have to take on debt to graduate?
- Will it allow me access to great opportunities in my field after I graduate?
- What kind of experiences does it offer for students—internships with local companies or non-profits, study-abroad opportunities, service trips, intramurals, unique electives?

While there is a place for rankings, and they do spotlight some of the top colleges, research prospective schools on the elements that are important to *you*. At the end of the day, you need to find the one that will enable you to thrive, no matter its spot on a list!

Rank Isn't Everything

Angie Sun had a decision to make.

She had been accepted into her dream school, Massachusetts Institute of Technology (MIT), a prestigious institution ranked in the Top 10 by *US News & World Report*. Unfortunately, her dream school didn't offer her any financial aid or scholarships. She would have to pay nearly $70,000 per year to attend! She was also accepted by Michigan State University, which offered her a full-ride scholarship.

On decision day, she informed her mom that she had decided on MIT. Angie was shocked when her mom said no. Angie had worked extremely hard throughout high school to earn a spot on MIT's acceptance list, a spot she believed was necessary in order to achieve her career aspirations. It felt like all her hard work was for nothing, her future hopes shattered.

Eventually, Angie realized it wasn't the school name on her degree that would determine her success. She decided to make the most of her free public-school education and create opportunities for herself. Because of her determination, she was able to graduate in three years instead of four and land her dream job at the number one workplace in the country, Google! All without taking on any debt!

"You are the magic in the equation, not the prestigious university," she says. "As long as you work for it, you'll get the career and the future you deserve. You don't need an Ivy-brand stamp on your résumé to show the world how amazing you are." Angie Sun's experience definitely represents that truth.

College ROI

Rather than ranking schools based simply on prestige and quality of education, many college guides are now starting to classify them by return on investment—analyzing which schools will profit you most, based on your projected lifetime earnings. To do this, they consider things like the level of debt their students graduate with and alumni salaries.

PayScale.com has ranked nearly 1,500 colleges, both public and private, in this way. PayScale also lists specific majors and the starting salaries of graduates from each of these schools. So if you're concerned about how much college will cost you compared to what you can expect to make in your lifetime, sites like this will give you an idea.

To determine your own ROI for a particular school, below are some of the top factors to consider:

The price published in a college brochure is often very different from what a student ends up paying. A more effective measure of a school's actual cost is its net price. To figure this number, you take the entire cost of attendance—including room and board, books, and expenses—and subtract any potential grants or scholarships. Schools that receive federal aid (which is most colleges and universities) are required to have a net price calculator on their website to help you know the true cost of attending.

When using these calculators, keep in mind that they are typically set for in-state students; out-of-state students may not get estimates that are as accurate. Also, the net price numbers are based on the first year of college only. There may be differences between freshman year and the following years that need to be accounted for. Having this number, though, will at least help you get a more accurate picture of the cost of a college *for you*, enabling you to figure out how much you'll need to cover.

FOUR-YEAR COMPLETION RATE

This technical-sounding term simply means "length of time to graduate." A lot of students at colleges that claim to be four-year institutions take longer than four years to complete their degree. According to a study by the National Center for Education Statistics, only about 40 percent of first-time, full-time students actually finished their degree in four years! Around 20 percent needed four to six years, and the rest required more than six years or did not graduate at all.

Certainly there are many reasons for needing more time to complete one's degree. Sometimes it's personal circumstances or a change of goals rather than the school itself. On the other hand, school-controlled factors like the difficulty of scheduling needed classes or a lack of guidance from advisors can lead to longer stints on campus. So if graduating in four years is a priority for you, pay attention to the completion rate at the colleges you are considering—especially since, as we've already discussed, "the longer you stay, the more you pay." If you think it'll take you more than four years to graduate, factor in the net price of those additional semesters (or years) when calculating the overall cost of your education.

EARNING POTENTIAL

Getting a ballpark estimate of what you'll make after graduation is important in the ROI equation. While it's impossible to predict your exact income, PayScale.com annually releases data on salary potential at various universities.

Having a good idea of your future earnings will help you make better decisions about the appropriate amount to spend on your degree. If your graduating salary as an engineer will be $65,000, paying more to attend a prestigious institution may be an appropriate investment. However, if you plan to be a social worker and the average starting salary is $35,000, that extra $100,000 for a private school probably doesn't make as much sense.

Now is the time to really explore whether the expensive private degree is the way for you to go, or if you can get similar results at a less expensive school. Because, again, at the end of the day, a degree is an investment, and you want to do your best to ensure your investment pays off.

ROI Gone Bad

I recently heard a radio interview with one of my favorite financial gurus, Dave Ramsey. He spoke with a lady who went $175,000 into student loan debt in order to become a teacher. At the time of the phone call, her annual salary was $38,500. You could hear the desperation in her voice as she struggled to figure out how she would ever get out from under that burden. Mr. Ramsey was quite frustrated that she took on that debt in the first place, given the limited earning potential for her field.

While it's totally acceptable, and in many cases respectable, to pick a major and a career path that doesn't earn a high salary, don't strap yourself with education debt that will take your entire life to pay off.

OPPORTUNITY COST

We talked about opportunity cost in chapter 1. When thinking through this in an educational capacity, it's basically a matter of weighing missed income against the value of a degree. This is especially relevant for people who are considering advanced degrees. If your starting salary after a bachelor's degree would be around $50,000 but you're considering continuing on to a full-time master's degree program that costs $35,000 per year, will that two-year degree be worth the $100,000 in lost income and an additional $70,000 in school fees? There's a good chance the answer will be yes. The higher earning potential of a graduate degree may well justify the investment. But evaluating the numbers beforehand can give you a true picture for your decision-making process.

Knowing college ROIs and where to find them is a good thing, but it's not the *only* thing. Students evaluate and select colleges for a variety of reasons including location, culture, program quality, family alma mater . . . and the list goes on and on. So keep ROI in mind as you are deciding which college to attend, but make your choice based on the school that best suits your educational and personal needs. Ultimately, it will be *you* and your motivation that will ensure your success and happiness.

Find the Most Merit Aid

Unfortunately, many families with talented, hard-working students either receive far less financial aid than they need, or (in fewer cases) don't qualify for financial aid at all based on their FAFSA. And that is where merit-based aid can really help fill in the gap, providing students with free money based on their track record.

There are many ways to earn merit aid, both from colleges and universities as well as private organizations and scholarship funds. So how do you find the most generous schools with the greatest likelihood of offering you merit aid?

CHECK THE STATS

Various publications and websites have gathered extensive data on college financing at a multitude of colleges and universities that can be used to make informed decisions about your possibilities of receiving aid at a particular school. CollegeData.com's search tool allows you to find colleges offering the highest amount of merit aid by ranking them in order from most generous to least. *US News & World Report* provides a similar list. Search for the statistics on each college you plan to apply to so you can get an idea of how much money you may be offered and what your true cost of attendance will be.

DON'T COUNT ON IVY LEAGUES
OR OTHER TOP SCHOOLS

Most elite schools don't offer merit-based scholarships. Why not? It's the law of supply and demand at work. The competition to get in is so great that they don't need to offer discounts and incentives to incoming students—they already have people in line willing to pay full price. On the other hand, smaller, lesser-known private colleges tend to offer more generous merit-based aid to students in order to remain competitive. Many of these "more generous" schools still have great academics and high earning potential for graduates.

Before applying, visit each college's website and run its net price calculator to determine the amount of merit-based scholarships you might receive. With some calculators, you can see what impact varying grades and test scores will have on merit offers. While potential merit aid is not always properly reflected in the net price calculations, you should at least get some idea of what to expect.

APPLY, APPLY, APPLY

Be willing to look beyond your comfort zone when applying for college. You may be set on one or two top schools, but try to keep an open mind and apply for others that may offer more merit aid. You're not committing to anything with this strategy, but rather, giving yourself the best chance at receiving a great offer and graduating debt-free.

SEARCH FOR POSSIBILITIES

While some merit-based awards are distributed simply as a result of data collected on admission applications, many of them require a few extra steps: through auditions or competitions prior to campus arrival, applications focused on a specific major, or separate scholarship applications on the school's website. For colleges and universities you're seriously considering, research additional merit-based scholarship opportunities beyond their admission application.

Alternate Routes

There are many paths to earning a college education. While you may have become more familiar with "traditional" four-year experiences, pursuing alternate routes can offer tremendous savings while still getting you to your destination. Keep an open mind as we explore these possibilities.

ONLINE DEGREES

Online education has become an increasingly popular option for earning a college degree. Every year new schools are being started, and more established ones are improving their offerings. They come with a host of benefits that can help slash college costs, including:

- *Low-cost tuition.* Many online schools offer tuition rates that are significantly lower than on-campus rates. While there is no universal equation for how online schools charge (per semester versus per credit hour versus lump sum), many keep rates low to compete with traditional universities.
- *Financial aid.* In 2006, Congress passed a bill that paved the way for online students to apply for and receive federal financial assistance. You can access the possibilities by submitting your FAFSA.
- *Lower COA.* The cost of attendance is lower online than at a traditional university because there's no need for housing or meal plans. As mentioned in chapter 6, these plans average $10,000 or more per year. The ability to be location-independent lets you find the most affordable way to live while you complete your education.
- *Flexibility.* Many programs are self-paced, meaning you can adapt your education to accommodate your schedule, letting you more easily maintain a job and pay as you go.

If you're juggling other commitments like full-time work or parenting, online school may be the ideal way to strike a balance and save money. Of course, do your research and thoroughly evaluate each program. It's important to understand what your total costs will be, including any fees, and what your opportunities for transferring credit would be should you ever need to change programs.

Online Made It Possible

In February 2011, Bobby Watkins decided to pursue his bachelor's degree in criminal justice. He was 32 years old, had a full-time job, three children—and he had not attended school in 14 years. Though he had no college credits, he signed up with an online university and dove right in.

Finding time to fit in his schooling was difficult. His ever-changing schedule ensured that he never worked the same hours from one day to the next. He and his wife had two children still in diapers, and she worked full time as well. He was also coaching his son's football team—all the while completing his coursework. And yet, the flexibility of the online format made it possible. "Although it was overwhelming at times, it was worth it," he says.

Bobby was fortunate that the college he attended recognized the value of his work experience and gave him 24 credit hours before he even started taking classes. It took him three years to complete the program, but in the end, he was able to get his bachelor's degree. He was the first person in his family to earn a college degree—in his words: "forever changing the shape of my family tree."

COMMUNITY COLLEGE

You may want to consider attending a community college and then transferring to a four-year program. At the end of a bachelor's degree, you'd still graduate with the same diploma as your peers who went all four years. However, with the average tuition and fees at a community college being just under $3,500 (according to the College Board), this possibility offers massive savings over attending a four-year school during that initial two-year period. Before moving forward with this option though, make sure the credits from your two-year program will transfer to the college you have in mind.

If you are working your way through school, having an associate's degree may also help you get a higher-paying job while you complete the remainder of your four-year degree. For example, a two-year associate's in computer programming could equip you to work part-time as a programmer. Even if you plan to continue your schooling to become a computer engineer, this would be a great career stepping-stone as you complete your bachelor's. Plus, you'd gain valuable experience in your chosen field.

US ARMED FORCES

An abundance of college-related funding is available to members of the various branches of the armed forces. I've highlighted some of the biggest ones below:

- *Military schools.* The military provides many types of colleges and academies to its men and women in exchange for a period of service after graduation. Enrollees don't pay tuition, and some receive benefits like free books, housing, and a stipend. Additionally, certain individuals get promoted, graduating not just with a degree but also a higher rank.
- *GI Bill.* This program provides tuition and living allowances for up to 36 months of schooling to service members and veterans, or their dependents, according to the length of time in active duty. Qualified individuals have up to 15 years to use their GI Bill benefits.
- *ROTC.* Various branches of the ROTC, or Reserve Officers' Training Corps, offer participants free college tuition and fees, a book allowance, and monthly stipends in exchange for a commitment to serve full time for four years.
- *Tuition assistance.* Active-duty personnel may be eligible for tuition help based on credit hours, up to a yearly cap.

- *Scholarships.* Many private organizations offer substantial awards to active military, veterans, and their spouses and/or dependents via competitive application processes.
- *State and college offers.* Some states and schools grant varying benefits to service members, ranging from discounts to scholarships to full tuition breaks. For example, the College Fee Waiver for Veteran Dependents program in California makes it possible for the children of America's servicemen and -women to attend any of its state community colleges or universities at no cost.

If serving our country and getting an education is in your vision, there's a tremendous amount of funding available to help you along the way. What I've highlighted above only scratches the surface. You can find out more at your local armed forces recruiting office.

Majors That Count

Deciding on a college major is a big decision. It requires you to put a stake in the sand and declare, "This is where I'm going!" That may feel super intimidating to you, or you may be somebody who chooses not to worry over it, figuring you'll fall into something when the time is right. Finding a balance between those two positions is ideal. You shouldn't be frantic, but at the same time, it's important to take the decision seriously.

There's a lot that goes into choosing a major. First and foremost, there's the personal element. You want to select something that will engage you, not only throughout college but possibly for your entire career. While classes can be challenging regardless of your major, some will appeal more to your personal interests and the way your brain works than others. Learning gets more fun in college, because you get to choose your own path and study things that excite you.

Beyond the personal aspect of picking a major, it's also important to weigh the long-term career and financial prospects associated with a field of study. As we've discussed, a college degree is a significant investment. And as with all investments, you want to evaluate your projected return and make sure it aligns with your financial goals.

Don't stress about your major, but do be proactive in your approach. It's a big decision that can significantly set your course for future success.

Let's discuss some important things to evaluate when picking a major.

YOUR "WHY"

The most obvious and critical starting point is evaluating why you are considering a certain major. Are you passionate about the field of study? Have you always envisioned a particular job? Do you like the financial prospects? There are a host of reasons that students pursue a certain major. While there is no wrong answer, it is important to make sure the major truly fits your reason for considering it. For any field you have in mind, do your research and get to know what the educational path will look like as well as the typical career outcomes. Speak to people who have completed that program, and learn about their experiences both at school and in the workplace.

Also, make sure you are considering the major for YOU. It's not uncommon for students to feel pressure from family or friends to choose a certain major. Perhaps several of your family members are in a certain field, but you're not sure it's right for you. Or you've always felt pushed to pursue a high-paying career, but you've been interested in non-profit or social work. While advice and insights can be helpful, you have to choose what is right for you.

REQUIREMENTS

Get to know the academic requirements for your potential major. What are the classes you'll need to complete that degree, and what is their level of difficulty? The course catalog will lay them all out with descriptions, so you can get a better understanding of what this particular road will be like.

You want to avoid getting two or three years into your

program and then switching because you didn't properly assess what was ahead. Research by Complete College America reveals that, on average, students take 16.5 hours over what they need to complete their bachelor's degree. If you're paying for college out of pocket, that extra semester's worth of credit is time *and* money—two of your most important resources. So you want to be strategic and take only the classes you need to graduate.

First, make sure you not only enjoy the major but will be excited about the classes that come with it. Some students pick a program based on an ideal, only to learn that the day-to-day subject matter is a far cry from what they expected. Second, it may seem obvious, but you should honestly evaluate whether the requirements fit your abilities and skill set. You might be considering mechanical engineering because you love cars, but if you've always struggled with math and science, you may want to steer clear of a major that's loaded with these types of courses. Just because a program is difficult doesn't mean you should avoid it, but do make sure you understand what you're getting into before you commit—and that you're up for the challenge.

PROGRAM STRENGTH

Not all college programs are created equal—even highly ranked schools can have departments that are not very strong. Likewise, lesser-known colleges may be nationally recognized in one particular major. Keep this in mind both when picking a college and choosing a specific major.

A few signs of a potentially weak program are:

- Very few faculty members
- Primarily part-time faculty
- Faculty members without advanced degrees in the field
- Minimal course offerings

If, prior to college, you have a good sense of what you want to major in, you'll be that much better equipped to choose a school with a reputation for excellence in your area of focus. If you're already in college and have discovered that the department you're in is lacking, don't panic. Instead, explore alternative majors with stronger programs that might allow you to reach the same career outcome. You may not find a better solution, but switching schools should be a last option, not a first step.

CAREER OPPORTUNITY

When evaluating majors, don't stop at the curriculum and course requirements. Look into the career prospects. What types of jobs does this course of study typically lead to, and do they appeal to you? Many students choose majors simply because they like the subject area, but they don't really think through the kind of work they'll be doing after graduation. For example, you may love political science as a subject, but not enjoy the idea of government service or election campaign work, which are the most common jobs for graduates with this degree. Make sure the major you select can lead to a job you'll enjoy.

Another factor to consider is how abundant the job opportunities are for graduates with your major. A degree is only useful if you have a workplace to use it in. Examine market trends to see what the industry might look like when you graduate. Is the field growing? Is the job market booming for your major, or is it oversaturated? You want to pick a course of study that gives you the best chance possible of landing a great job after graduation.

Also find out: Is there more than one major that could lead to your dream job? You may assume that studying finance is the best route to being a corporate chief financial officer someday, when in fact research by BusinessInsider .com shows that among the 100 top-earning CFOs they surveyed, almost 20 percent earned their bachelor's in business administration rather than finance (less than 5 percent). For many careers, there is more than one major that can get you there. My friend who ended up in publishing (see page 123) looked at creative writing, English, journalism, literature, and communications as potential courses of study. Any of them would've opened the door to her dream. Do the research to fully understand your options before you decide.

········
TIMING
········

Once you're on campus and registering for your first semester of classes, you may feel some pressure to declare your major right away. But if you're unsure about what you want to spend the next several years studying, hold off. It's never a good idea to rush a life-altering decision. According to the National Center for Education Statistics, about four out of five of America's college students end up changing their major at least once. So it's not uncommon to be uncertain. There's nothing wrong with patiently yet proactively exploring the options so you can make a more effective decision down the road. In the meantime, you can take classes that meet your general requirements and still count toward your degree.

On the other hand, if you do know with complete certainty what you want to study, there are some perks, such as being able to pick a college or university with a top program in your field. You can also plan your four-year curriculum with much more intentionality, avoiding an extended stay in school. Additionally, you can be much more focused with internships and other work experiences as you build your résumé.

Find Your Fit

Be open to exploring and evaluating various options that may lead to financially freeing results. There are ways to make any education top quality while still graduating debt-free. Students from all kinds of educational backgrounds—including those from lesser-known schools—end up in the halls of Google, on Wall Street, and in the most competitive workplaces.

Don't automatically accept society's norm as being *your* norm. An excellent education is not just about attending the best school or following the most popular path. It's about finding your fit.

SUMMARY POINTS

▶ There's a lot more to a college than where it falls on the list of popular rankings. Explore prospective schools in-depth, keeping in mind key factors that are important to you.

▶ Many college guides are now starting to classify schools by ROI, analyzing which schools will profit you most, based on your projected lifetime earnings.

▶ To find the most generous schools with the greatest likelihood of offering you merit aid: check the stats, look beyond top colleges, apply to multiple schools, and search for additional possibilities.

- Pursuing alternate routes to a college education—for example, online schools, community colleges, and the US armed forces—can offer tremendous savings toward earning your degree.

- Consider these important factors when picking a major that counts: your "why," the course requirements, program strength, and the career opportunities it affords.

9

BUDGET AND SAVE
Making Your Money Stretch

Don't tell me what you value.
Show me your budget,
and I'll tell you what you value.

Joseph R. Biden

It's no secret that the majority of college students are pretty broke. It's a point in life when you're seriously investing in your future and preparing for great returns down the road . . . and yet you're not making a lot of money. So how do you pay your bills, save, and still have fun during these minimal-income years?

A lot of students would prefer to avoid the first two parts of that question and simply focus on the last: "still have fun." Unfortunately, not addressing all three parts together can land you where so many college graduates have ended up: lamenting that they could have saved more and borrowed less while in school.

Learning to create a budget and be on top of your finances during the college years can positively affect you for the rest of your life. That's how important it is. For students who are right out of high school, it's typically the first time in their lives that their financial health and freedom are completely their responsibility.

Whether you're getting support from your parents or flying solo, learning to manage your income and budget now will help you start building the financially sound future you're aspiring to. Done correctly, you can pay, save, *and* still have fun.

Set Goals

The first thing I'd recommend before setting up your budget is establishing goals. Maintaining a budget can be tedious at times, and you need to know why you're doing it. What is your purpose for diligently tracking your finances, especially when you look around and see that many of your peers don't really seem to care?

Your goal could simply be to stay out of debt. If you search YouTube for terms like *student debt crisis*, you'll hear countless devastating stories of individuals who got themselves into crippling debt during college. Time and again, they share how much it's hurt them and the consequent challenges they're facing today. Perhaps that could be your motivation: realizing how common it is to graduate with a mountain of student loan debt, and doing everything you can now to enjoy as much financial freedom as possible after college.

Or perhaps your goal is to graduate with a certain amount of savings, or to take an amazing trip abroad to celebrate getting your degree. Whatever it is that motivates you, find it and focus on it. You'll likely need that push when your friends are all going dress shopping for the third sorority formal of the year, or they want you to go on a spring break trip you know is much more than you can afford. You'll have plenty of chances to buy amazing clothes and go on fantastic vacations in the future if you manage your money effectively; and trust me, it feels so much better when you don't have to stress about it!

How to Set a Budget

TIMING

The first thing to do is determine the time frame for your budget. What will be your parameters, and how often will you revisit your figures? For full-time students, it's typically best to break down your budget by semester and then track and re-evaluate it each month. A few reasons why this works:

- A lot of the biggest expenses students face will vary from semester to semester. The bills also tend to stack up seasonally, particularly at the beginning of a semester. Therefore, projecting in smaller segments of time will help you more realistically prepare. Among the things you'll have to account for are books, room and board, student activity fees, and trips home—and those things could vary by several hundred dollars, depending on the month.

- If you're relying on money from other sources (scholarships, grants, student loans, or your relatives) to fund expenses, you'll likely receive that money in a lump sum to cover an entire semester. When you get the cash all at once, it can seem like a lot and there's no need to worry. However, you need to budget so you don't spend it too quickly and end up falling short at semester's end.

- If a part-time job is your primary source of funds, looking at the entire semester will help you save up for those variable expenses that don't come every month but that you still need to plan for.

If your school is set up on quarters or trimesters, then take these principles and adjust accordingly. Or if it will help you handle your money better, consider setting up a monthly budget for yourself regardless of your school's schedule.

And don't forget this: while budgeting for each semester, be sure to keep in mind the expenses that are on the horizon and save up for them. For example, if you're paying for books out of pocket by working a part-time job, arrange to have enough reserved in December to cover the bills that will come due in January when the new semester starts. Once you've created your overall semester budget, it's pretty easy to establish short-term goals and track your monthly expenses.

···········

METHOD

···········

There are many ways you can manage your budget—most of them dependent on your personal preferences and style. Some students use a spreadsheet; some lean on the variety of budget-managing apps and tech tools available on the market, and still others like the simple paper-and-pen method. The key here is to find what works for you. Make sure it's something you'll feel comfortable looking back at regularly. If it's confusing or impractical, you'll be less likely to use it.

I personally prefer a simple Excel file that I've created. There are many templates available online, even ones specifically intended for college students. Some examples of online budget management tools are:

- Mint.com
- YouNeedABudget.com
- BudgetPulse.com
- BudgetSimple.com
- BudgetTracker.com

Whatever helps you be the most organized and effective is what's best. Explore the options, and if you happen to pick one that isn't clicking for you, try another one the next semester. You have many years of budget excellence ahead of you, so take the time to figure it out now.

GET TO THE NUMBERS

Income

Now it's time to assess how much total money you will have coming in during your budget period and then break it down by month or week. (See the chart below.) You'll want to consider things like:

- *Income from work.* Estimate how much money you'll be making from your job, and if your hours will vary, estimate low, just so you're covered. Should you end up working more hours than anticipated—then bonus!—you can get that much further ahead! If you plan on earning most of your money for school during the summer months, you may want to estimate your total summer pay, then divide it by 12 to account for each month throughout the year.
- *Income from financial aid.* Total up any refund money you'll have coming in from sources like scholarships, grants, work-study, and loans. Some students receive

these funds to take care of expenses beyond tuition. This is allowed, up to your school's official cost of attendance. Again, be sure to divide these lump-sum payments in your budget to cover multiple months.

- *Parent or family contribution.* Family members may be giving you some sort of allowance or assistance toward bills or college expenses. Include this income in your budget as well.

Income	
Summer Job	$4,000/12 = $333 per month
Estimated Fall Financial Aid Refund	$1,500/4 months = $375 per month
Allowance from Grandparents	$100
Part-Time Job	$600
Total Monthly Income: $1,408	

Expenses

Next, you want to factor in the money that goes out. It's important to track and organize all your expenses to make sure they do not exceed the amount you make. Go through all your projected costs—semester school fees and living expenses—and include them.

Think through the numbers in this way:

- *Fixed expenses.* These stay the same from month to month and tend to be non-negotiable. They can include things like rent, car payment, and insurance. Since you know the price in advance, you know exactly how much of your budget will fall under this category each month.
- *Variable expenses.* These are costs that can change from month to month, such as groceries/meals, shopping, and entertainment. Variable expenses can be both the easiest to control and the most common budget busters. It's easy to drop a few dollars on new music, a shirt here and there, or snacks while out with friends, and then not understand how you went over budget that month. To stay on track, create categories of variable expenses and then set the maximum you will spend in each area.

As tiresome as it may sound, write down or use an app to track all your spending in detail, at least for a period of time, to better understand your habits and where your money goes. This will enable you to set a realistic amount for each category of expenses and have a great idea of where you can cut back as you need to.

Finding the Balance

Now bring the numbers together to determine your budget. Simply subtract your expenses from your income to find the difference. If you have a positive balance—great! That means you're spending less than you're earning, which is where you want to be. Rather than going out and spending more, be wise with the extra and contribute to savings. Or if you've accumulated any debt, start paying it down.

On the other hand, if your expenses exceed your income, you'll know that something needs to be adjusted downward, because you are spending more than you can afford. Try to reduce your variable expenses, cut back on fixed expenses, or earn more money (see chapter 2). Of course, it's typically easier to cut back than to increase income, so really evaluate your expenditures and see what you can reduce or eliminate entirely. We'll talk further about money-saving tips coming up in this chapter.

Keep in mind the importance of saving up for emergencies and unexpected expenses as well. Especially as a college student on a tight budget, it can be hard to deal with unanticipated hits like needing to travel home for a family emergency or having your car break down. Set a little money aside each month to fund these types of costs. Put this away first, so you're not tempted to spend it.

Let's look at a sample budget:

Monthly Income: $1,408	
Fixed Expenses	Variable Expenses
Savings $100	Gas $100
Rent $450	Food $300
Car $200	Recreation $125
Insurance $75	
Phone $50	
Total Expenses: $1,400	
Total Income ($1,408) - Total Expenses ($1,400) = $8	

Take the time to regularly review and maintain your budget—at least monthly, though weekly works best for a lot of people. Keeping track of your income and spending ensures that you are moving toward your goals and that there aren't any surprises.

Making Your Money Stretch

Every dollar counts, and any opportunity to save a few can definitely help. That's true for everybody, but especially college students! When funds are limited, you may have to be a little creative, but it's still possible to enjoy a great life-style. So let's talk about how to make the money you *do* have stretch as far as possible.

PRIORITIZE

College is a blast, and there are a lot of things *worth* spending money on if you have it. From social events and nights out, to paying activity fees and taking trips, the possibilities are virtually endless. The problem comes when you try to do them all, quickly draining your bank account. The answer is to prioritize, finding ways to save *for* the things that are most important to you and save *from* the things that don't matter as much.

Whatever your priorities are, remember them as motivation when you're tempted to overspend on something that isn't that big of a deal. For example, while I love a good white chocolate mocha, spending $5 a day at Starbucks adds up to $1,825 per year. With that money, I could easily do something that is a bigger priority to me, like go on a fun trip with friends.

For you, maybe that money could go toward paying fraternity dues or saving up for a car. Ask yourself, *What's "worth it" for me?* Then use that as a filter as you think through each purchase.

TAKE ADVANTAGE OF BEING A STUDENT

There are numerous discounts available to students just for flashing their student IDs or for having a .*edu* e-mail address. Many retail stores like Banana Republic and Kate Spade will give students 10 to 15 percent off purchases. Several thrift stores also offer discount days for students. You can save several hundreds of dollars on Apple products by receiving their education pricing, plus even more if your state has a back-to-school, tax-free weekend. And many restaurants like Arby's and Subway extend students 10 percent off. Also, you can usually enjoy musicals, symphonies, and other live performances at local venues on a discount.

When it comes to purchasing anything off campus, it's almost always worth asking if they give students a discount. What do you have to lose? The worst they'll say is no, and there's a great chance you'll end up getting to keep some cash in your pocket.

MAKE THE MOST OF YOUR
MEAL PLAN OR NIX IT

Most college meal plans aren't cheap. When you break down the cost, many plans are over $10 per meal. As you decide on the right option for you, try to think through the reality of how much you'll eat in the dining hall and what cheaper alternatives may be nearby. Getting breakfast or lunch for under $10 off campus or through grocery shopping isn't usually that difficult; therefore, be strategic when picking your meal plan and really think through if the costs are worth it.

If you do pick a meal plan, make the most of your investment. It's not uncommon for students to reach the end of the semester realizing that several meals went to waste. Even if you are in a hurry or intend to eat off campus that day, your dining hall most likely has a carryout option. Grab a meal to take with you, and keep it stored in a dorm refrigerator. You've already paid for it, so you might as well use it.

GET CHEAP BOOKS

The College Board estimates that the average cost of books and supplies is $1,298 per year at a four-year public school. Most of your books will be used for one semester, only to be replaced by equally expensive ones the next semester. Don't simply accept the sticker price at the university store. Do some research to see if you can find a better deal somewhere else. Price-comparison engines like CampusBooks.com allow students to see the best available quotes for renting and buying new, used, and digital books.

Once you're done with your books, why not resell them?

College bookstores will generally buy back used copies if the edition is still current. You can also look into posting them online at textbook-buying sites like BookScouter.com and Textbookrush.com, or selling directly to a peer using Amazon, craigslist, Facebook, a campus bulletin board—or simply by word of mouth.

DO FREE STUFF

On a tight budget, recreational spending needs to be limited, but that doesn't mean you can't still have a great time! Fortunately, there's a wealth of opportunity on or near most college campuses. Pay attention to flyers around campus and e-mail newsletters for free on-campus events. You'll not only have the opportunity to meet new people and become more involved in your campus community, but many events offer food and fun perks. Also, look for free activities in your college town. From local street festivals to live concerts to bowling nights for students, many towns offer outings that cost nothing or very little and are a blast. If anything, it could be a worthwhile challenge to just try something different rather than doing the usual (such as going to a movie). You're not likely to be the only one of your friends on a budget, so put your heads together and come up with fun plans for cheap.

Study abroad. Spring break. Weekend getaways. Family visits. College students travel for all kinds of reasons! If traveling is a priority to you, as it is for many students, take advantage of the variety of discounts online. If you know where to look and how to navigate the deals, you can save hundreds and see the world!

Here are some great ways to save:

- *Student discount sites.* Websites like StudentUniverse .com and STATravel.com have negotiated deals with various airlines, hotels, and tour companies to help students book trips at discounted rates.
- *Fare alerts.* On big purchases like airline tickets, you want to make sure you get the best price available. Setting up alerts allows you to monitor fares for dates and destinations of your choice and be notified when the price reaches a low point. Airfarewatchdog.com and Kayak.com are currently the most popular sites for price alerts, though there are others available online.
- *Deal aggregators.* Travel sales come up every day on numerous websites. To find the best ones, use online aggregators, which comb through the various sites out

there to bring you the best and most up-to-date deals. Top websites for this include TravelZoo.com and DealNews.com's travel and entertainment section.

- *Hotel alternatives.* Consider lower-price accommodations by using websites like Airbnb.com, Couchsurfing.com, and Homestay.com, which allow you to stay in someone's home, often for less than you'd pay at a hotel. Plus, you get a unique chance to appreciate local culture. Of course, thoroughly read the reviews and research the neighborhood of each place to ensure safety and a pleasant experience.

- *Cost splitting.* Whether it's hitching a ride over break with another student from your hometown, flying to a destination and sharing accommodations, or just a good old-fashioned road trip, splitting travel costs is a great way to save money. Smartphone apps like Venmo and Square Cash make sharing payments simpler.

While traveling is considered more of a luxury, it doesn't necessarily have to be out of reach. With planning and determination, you can be among the adventurers who have found crazy deals that allowed them to travel for ridiculously cheap.

AVOID UNNECESSARY FEES

Make a habit of paying your bills on time to avoid wasting money on late fees. If your bank offers online bill pay, sign up and keep things simple. Remember to regularly check your bank balance, ensuring that all payments have gone through as scheduled. Also, to protect your identity so you don't fall prey to identity thieves, avoid logging into your bank account on a public computer. If you absolutely must, make sure to log out and to clear the web browser immediately after use.

Heads-Up

Some people take a head-in-the-sand approach and avoid facing their financial picture until they encounter a major problem. This can only lead to trouble. It's far better to notice any issues in your budget and fix them immediately before they become bigger.

If you *do* make a regrettable spending decision one month, or if you forget to include some line item in your budget, forgive yourself and move ahead. Your goal is not perfection—it's diligence. And you'll see your diligence pay off when you graduate in a great financial position, without the worry of debt!

SUMMARY POINTS

▶ Before establishing your budget, first set goals to remind you of your purpose for tracking your finances. This work can be tedious at times, and you need to know why you're doing it.

▶ When developing your budget: decide on a time frame, pick a method for managing your budget, evaluate the numbers, and then find your balance.

▶ To make the money you do have stretch as far as possible: prioritize, take advantage of being a student, make the most of your meal plan or nix it, get cheap books, do free stuff, travel for less, and avoid unnecessary fees.

Conclusion
FREEDOM!

Part of me wishes I could say I had my plan completely worked out . . . but the truth is, I didn't. As I walked across the stage to receive my college degree, I still wasn't 100 percent certain what I wanted to do with my life.

When the offer came for a cushy corporate position, I thought, *I* should *take this* . . . It was an ideal job that paid an incredible starting salary and had all the perks I'd been hoping for, but for me, something didn't feel quite right.

I had been working toward the dream of writing a book for about six months. I planned to put it up on Amazon as a small eBook and then move on with my career. Yet I couldn't shake the feeling that there might be more to it. So I took a risk. I turned down the job and set out on my quest to become an author.

To be honest, it was a pretty scary decision. As a writer, there are no guarantees that anyone will want to read your work or that you'll be able to make a living. But here's the thing . . . I had the *freedom* to make that choice because I didn't have a mountain of student debt dictating my decision. And really, that's the point of *this* whole book. I want *you* to have the freedom to make choices with your future too.

To pick a job based on what you feel is right for you, not just one that covers your student loan bill.

To launch a business, travel the world, or invest in further education.

To celebrate getting married, purchasing a home, and having children without feeling you need permission from your debtors.

For me, that freedom to write my first book launched me into a career beyond what I imagined was possible. For you, who knows the wonderful places your dream of an education will lead you, especially when you follow it debt-free! So embrace your freedom and don't ever let it go. It's a worthwhile fight that pays off for a lifetime.

This is your financial future, your freedom. You hold the keys. You call the shots. Make it everything you ever hoped for. And don't let anyone tell you, "You can't." I believe you *will!*

I look forward to hearing your success stories. Please write me at:

E-mail: NotGoingBroke@gmail.com
Address: PO Box 291951
Nashville, TN 37229

RESOURCES

Aaup.org

Actstudent.org

Bigfuture.collegeboard.org

Blog.ed.gov

Completecollege.org

Edvisors.com

Epi.org

Finaid.org

Ifap.ed.gov

Insidehighered.com

Irs.gov

Jff.org

Nacacnet.org

Naceweb.org

Nces.ed.gov

Ncjrs.gov

News.salliemae.com

Payscale.com

Sat.collegeboard.org

Savingforcollege.com

Studentaid.ed.gov

Ticas.org

Trends.collegeboard.org

Usa.gov

Usnews.com

Whitehouse.gov

These resources and many more were referenced in the writing of this book. For more information, including direct links to studies, please visit TheCollegeNinja.com.

ACKNOWLEDGMENTS

I feel very blessed to have an A+ team working with me on this book. Mark, thank you for negotiating so well on my behalf and for sharing your wisdom and expertise. Your efforts were seamless. I admire both your professionalism and the quality of person you are. To the Worthy team, I couldn't be more thrilled to be publishing another book with you. It feels like I'm not only working with all-stars but family. I'm so grateful for your care and support from day one, and I'm honored to be on this journey with you. Kris, I'm so grateful for the days and nights of brainstorming, countless hours of combing through page by page, and the many memories we've shared writing this book. You are not only a rock star as an editor but also such an incredible friend! And to all the people who've allowed me to interview and survey them, thank you so very, very much. Your insights helped lay the foundation for this book and guided the content in a profound way. I will forever be grateful for your wonderful contributions.

The process of writing this book would have been so much more difficult without the support of great friends. Writing for an extended length of time can sometimes feel a bit lonely, but your encouragement and love made it far easier to stay on course. Courtney, thank you so much for making the eight-hour drive from Chicago when I was feeling especially isolated. Having you sit and work with me for those few days recharged my battery in a powerful way! Suz, I really appreciate your willingness to spend time brainstorming and thinking through ideas with me. To my Bible study girls, I'm so grateful for your cheers and prayers. I feel very loved. And to the many other friends who have shared positive vibes and brought so much joy to this writing season—thank you. Your kind words and belief in me never go unnoticed. I absolutely adore having you in my life.

Last, but certainly not least, I want to thank my rocks . . . my foundation . . . my family. Mom, thank you for helping start this whole journey. Without your push and words of wisdom, I wouldn't be here today. The chances you took and the sacrifices you made are appreciated more than I can ever express. Slate, I'm so happy I get to do life with my best friend. The way you believe in me and truly support my goals and dreams is incredible—even going so far as to take time off of work to spend 16-hours-plus days combing through every word of this book with me. You definitely get "Husband of the Year" for this one! To Grandma, Grandpa, Mark, Jessi, the Sniders, Sherry, Gerry, and the many other members of our family who have prayed for me and surrounded me with love not just in this process but my entire life, thank you! I love you all so much!

INDEX

For more information on the author, visit:
KristinaEllis.com

Follow Kristina's tweets and Instagram posts
@MyKristinaEllis

To contact Kristina for speaking opportunities,
media requests, or interviews,
please send an e-mail to:
Info@KristinaEllis.com

Visit TheCollegeNinja.com

Find Helpful Tools, Information, and Inspiration

Scholarship Listings

Sample Scholarship Application Forms Tips & Tricks

Scholar Stories

Instructional Videos

And more!

You can subscribe to Kristina's e-mail list at
TheCollegeNinja.com

Also from
Kristina Ellis

9781617951572

IF YOU ENJOYED THIS BOOK, WILL YOU CONSIDER SHARING THE MESSAGE WITH OTHERS?

Mention the book in a blog post or through Facebook, Twitter, Pinterest, or upload a picture through Instagram.

Recommend this book to those in your small group, book club, workplace, and classes.

Head over to facebook.com/worthypublishing, "LIKE" the page, and post a comment as to what you enjoyed the most.

Tweet "I recommend reading #NotGoingBroke by @mykristinaellis /@worthypub"

Pick up a copy for someone you know who would be challenged and encouraged by this message.

Write a book review online.

Visit us at worthypublishing.com

twitter.com/worthypub

worthypub.tumblr.com

facebook.com/worthypublishing

pinterest.com/worthypub

instagram.com/worthypub

youtube.com/worthypublishing